"One of the first books I tell new writers to buy. It is indispensable, practical, readable, and fun to use. Buy this book before you write another word!"

— Dean Batali, TV Writer/Producer (*That '70s Show, Buffy the Vampire Slayer*)

"Required reading for any screenwriter who wants to be taken seriously by Hollywood. Can't imagine how there never has been a book like this before!"

— Elizabeth Stephen, President, Television; Executive Vice President, Motion Picture Production, Mandalay Television Pictures

"It doesn't matter how great your screenplay is if it looks all wrong. *The Hollywood Standard* is probably the most critical book any screenwriter who is serious about being taken seriously can own. For any writer who truly understands the power of making a good first impression, this comprehensive guide to format and style is priceless."

— Marie Jones, Book Reviewer, www.absolutewrite.com

"Christopher Riley just made my job tougher! Each year experienced producers screen out hundreds of scripts because the mistakes in form and organization reveal them to be the work of amateurs. But if those hopeful writers follow Riley's concise and knowledgeable advice, they're going to look like the best professionals in Hollywood."

— Robert W. Cort, Producer (*Save the Last Dance, Runaway Bride, Mr. Holland's Opus, The Hand That Rocks the Cradle, Three Men and a Baby, Outrageous Fortune*)

"In Hollywood, looks matter. Read *The Hollywood Standard* to ensure that your script not only gets in past the Hollywood bouncers, but turns heads when it gets there."

— Amy Snow, winner, 2004 ABC/Disney Screenwriting Fellowship

"Riley has succeeded in an extremely difficult task: he has produced a guide to screenplay formatting which is both entertaining to read and exceptionally thorough. Riley's clear style, authoritative voice and well-written examples make this book far more enjoyable than any formatting guide has a right to be. This is the best guide to script formatting ever, and it is an indispensable tool for every writer working in Hollywood."

— Wout Thielemans, *Screentalk*

"*The Hollywood Standard* isn't just a rulebook for formatting scripts — it's a translator that explains how to make the visions and words in your head come to life on a page. From incorporating text messages and emails to writing simultaneous dialogue, it offers simple, easy-to-follow directions that make your script not only readable, but dramatic. Any question you may have about how something should look on a page, this book answers it. Don't keep it on your bookshelf — keep it on your desk."

— Chad Gervich, TV writer/producer (*Reality Binge, Foody Call, Speeders*), author of the best-selling book *Small Screen, Big Picture: A Writer's Guide to the TV Business*

"Christopher Riley has demystified screenplay format in his new edition of *The Hollywood Standard*. Screenwriters should read this from cover to cover and take notes because, in this crazy business where a writer's creative work can be disqualified because words are in the wrong places on the page, this book might save your career."

— Mary J. Schirmer, screenwriter, writing instructor, film critic

"A craftsman often bends the rules, an artist often breaks them. But to do it well, one must first know what those rules are, and I can think of no better way to learn them than Christopher Riley's *The Hollywood Standard*."

— Bill Marsilii, screenwriter, *Deja Vu*

"For years, while Christopher Riley was on the other side of the lot in the script department, standardizing feature formatting, we on the television side relished the lack of reliable formatting information. As we waded through piles and piles of Warner Bros. Workshop submissions, the look of a script was one of our secret short-cuts for separating the rookies from the pros. Now people will know both *how* and *why* television scripts are formatted. Thanks a lot, Chris..."

— Jack Gilbert, Warner Bros. Workshop

"A key insider Hollywood truism is that a screenplay is half-sold by presentation alone. Christopher Riley's *The Hollywood Standard* presents both the industry standard guidelines and the true insider secret — that your script sells by the way your script reads, how it lays on the page. Riley shows how scripts come alive on the page. Mastering these skills will communicate the movie you envision, and separate you from the pack. His expertise is a gift to all screenwriters and filmmakers."

— Bobette Buster, adjunct professor, USC School of Cinematic Arts, international speaker on screenwriting

THE HOLLYWOOD STANDARD

THE COMPLETE AND AUTHORITATIVE GUIDE
TO SCRIPT FORMAT AND STYLE

Second Edition

CHRISTOPHER RILEY

MICHAEL WIESE PRODUCTIONS

Published by Michael Wiese Productions
12400 Ventura Blvd.
Suite 1111
Studio City, CA 91604
(818) 379-8799, (818) 986-3408 (FAX)
mw@mwp.com
www.mwp.com

Cover design by MWP
Interior design by William Morosi
Copyedited by Paul Norlen
Printed by Sheridan Books, Chelsea, MI

Manufactured in the United States of America
Copyright 2009 by Christopher Riley

Library of Congress Cataloging-in-Publication Data

Riley, Christopher, 1961-
  The Hollywood standard : the complete and authoritative guide to script format and style / by Christopher Riley. –2nd ed.
    p. cm.
  Includes index.
  ISBN 978-1-932907-63-6
  1. Motion picture authorship--Handbooks, manuals, etc. 2. Authorship--Style manuals. I. Title.
  PN1996.R48 2009
  808.2'3--dc22

                                    2009009397

Printed on recycled stock

for Kathy, beautiful, brave and good

and for Rachel, Peter, Hope and Emily,
who make me smile

CONTENTS

ix

Unleashing the Power of Script Typing Software 154

FOREWORD

I've been a writer for a long time. I've been writing for well over 15 years. During all that time, I've discovered that writing a screenplay is a funny thing. You never get it right. It's like a math problem with a right answer, but you'll never get that answer. You can write and rewrite five or twelve or twenty-seven drafts and your answer might get better. But the best you can ever do is get a good answer, never a perfect answer.

I think that's because writing a screenplay is part art and part science. The art part of screenwriting comes naturally to me. The story. The characters. The action. But the science of screenwriting — the transitions, the parentheticals, the sluglines, all those tools the screenwriter uses to communicate the vision he has in his head — that part doesn't come naturally to me. For many years I didn't know how to use those elements. I knew what they were, of course, but I didn't feel I had mastered them. Sometimes I would envision a scene in my head and wonder, "How do I explain this? How do I put this scene on the page so other people will see the same scene that I see?"

When I began writing the script for *Training Day 2*, I decided I was going to get it right, both the art and the science. I wanted to write a script that was easy to read. A script that conveyed the film I had in my head simply and clearly. I was in a store in Los Angeles and saw the cover of this book, *The Hollywood Standard*. I picked it up and looked inside. It looked friendly. It looked simple. When I started reading it, I discovered it contained answers to questions I'd been asking while I was writing. I used this book to guide me through the process of writing that film. The positive response I got when the script was turned in to the studio wasn't solely a reflection of my talent for writing. It was a reflection of the fact that I'd written a script that read fluidly and in a format that people who read screenplays prefer. This book helped me communicate what I wanted to say.

A screenplay is like a map to a story. If you don't do it right, it won't tell the story you intended. Imagine writing a song. If you don't put the notes on the musical chart the way professional musicians are used to seeing them, they're not going to play the song you heard in your head and you're not going to be happy when you hear it. If you give a script to a studio that isn't written using standard Hollywood format, it may be a good idea, with good dialogue and action, but it doesn't come across the way you intended.

Aspiring writers sometimes wonder why people don't want to read their scripts. Sometimes it's not their story. Sometimes the format distracts. Sometimes scripts don't get passed up the chain because they're hard to read. I suspect that the fine points of screenplay format don't come naturally to anyone. They have to be learned. To write a screenplay, you need to learn the science. And this is the best, simplest, easiest to read book to teach you that science. It's the one I recommend to my students at UCLA. It's the one book I've found that addresses the questions I actually have. My copy is filled with sticky notes. I refer to it every day. I keep it beside my computer where I write. It's like having an assistant.

Did I say I keep one copy? The truth is I keep two. The one beside my computer, and the one in my briefcase, so that no matter where I am I always have it with me.

But I've realized that I really need three copies. Because I keep giving away the one in my briefcase. I give it to people I like. I give it to creative, smart, aspiring screenwriters. I give it because learning the art and science of screenwriting takes time. It takes years. And this book helps. So I give away the copy from my briefcase, then I go out and buy myself another one.

There are a few things you happen upon in this business that you never let go of. I have two things like that. One is my copy of Final Draft. And the other is *The Hollywood Standard*. And that's the truth.

Antwone Fisher

INTRODUCTION

Why a second edition?

Since publication of the first edition of *The Hollywood Standard* in 2005, film and television writers have embraced it as a reference they keep close at hand when they write. Many writers — both professionals and those who aspire to join the professional ranks — have told me they refer to this book every day. It has become for them a useful and even indispensable tool. I'm glad for that.

This second edition results from a desire to make a good book better.

The first major change? Michael Wiese, my astute publisher, suggested that the book might be more helpful if we printed it in 8.5-by-11-inch format, so that sample pages in the book would match the actual dimensions of a script page. Readers would then be able to lay their script pages side by side with the samples in the book to confirm the accuracy of their margins. I think it's a good idea and you can see that's what we've done. We've also used a special "lay flat" binding so that readers can easily work with the book while writing.

Next, I've added a series of new chapters at the beginning of the book to get writers off to a fast start. The book now launches with a "Quick Start Guide" introducing the fundamentals of standard script format, designed to get writers turning out professionally formatted pages in a hurry. After that comes a chapter titled "Avoiding a Dozen Deadly Formatting Mistakes," intended to help writers do precisely that. And, in response to questions from readers, I follow that up with a discussion of the differences between spec scripts and production drafts. Also in response to reader questions, I've added FAQs at the end of many of the chapters.

In the work of my students, I've seen the necessity of encouraging writers to proofread their work carefully, lest their creativity, attention to professional format and a million other details be dismissed by a reader who encounters a blizzard of typos. The problem is that effective proofreading is harder than it sounds. For that reason, I include a new chapter with tips for how to get it right.

Finally, because script format is an evolving discipline, I've updated the text in a variety of ways, including, for example, instructions about how to format things like email exchanges, caller ID readouts, instant messages and text message conversations.

What makes me such a know-it-all?

Fair question. Publishing a script format guide and calling it "standard," "complete" and "authoritative" takes a certain amount of chutzpah and has provoked a smidgen of criticism. Standard according to whom? How complete is complete? And by whose authority can it claim to be authoritative?

Like you, I'm a writer, so let me answer by way of a story.

Long, long ago, before even the first season of *ER*, I came to Hollywood to try my hand at screenwriting. Shortly after I arrived, I took a job proofreading scripts in Warner Bros.' acclaimed script processing department, in those days literally a 24-hour-a-day script factory. For fourteen years I worked alongside veterans the studio had lured away from Barbara's Place, the legendary Hollywood script house, learning and applying standard format rules to untold thousands of scripts. I ultimately ran the department as the historic studio's premier format guru. I wrote the script typing software the studio used to type countless scripts and served as the ultimate arbiter of format for that studio and for dozens of outside clients that included Amblin, Disney, Columbia, Universal, NBC Productions, Wilshire Court Productions, and many more. And, arguably, I ended up knowing as much about script format as anyone in Hollywood.

I've since found my way into the screenwriting career that lured me to Hollywood in the first place. With my wife and writing partner Kathy, I've walked the red carpet at the premier of our first film in Berlin. I've written movies for Touchstone and Paramount, Mandalay and Intermedia. I've also become a successful screenwriting instructor. And I've seen how badly we screenwriters need a reliable, easy-to-use format guide.

I originally wrote *The Hollywood Standard* to meet that need. The plan was to offer a guide based on my experience at Warner Bros., intended to be kept at a screenwriter's fingertips and filled with clear, concise, complete formatting instructions, and hundreds of examples to take the guesswork out of a multitude of formatting situations that perplex screenwriters, waste their time, and steal their confidence. Based on the response of screenwriters around the world, the first edition hit the spot for many of my fellow writers. I hope this new edition proves even more valuable.

"But I Don't Need a Book, I Use Final Draft"

Or Movie Magic Screenwriter. Or Scriptware. Or Celtx. Or one of the other incredibly useful and time-saving script typing programs on the market. What else does a writer need?

To begin with, standard format is about infinitely more than margins. It's knowing when to add a shot heading and when to leave one out. It's knowing how to get out of a POV shot and how to set up a montage. It's knowing what to capitalize and how to control pacing and what belongs in parenthetical character direction and whether those automatic (cont'd)s beside dialogue should be turned on or off. No script typing software is designed to answer those questions. Consequently, too many writers who think they're turning in professionally formatted screenplays are in fact often turning in scripts that brand them as amateurs.

The Fan Test

Stacks and stacks of scripts by first-timers and even professionals never receive serious consideration because they fail the fan test. Overworked readers, studio executives, agents, and producers pick up a script, flip to the last page and fan toward the front, looking at nothing but the physical layout of the script on the page. The format. What they see forms their first impression of your dream script. And sometimes their last. This guide tells you want you need to know to get your script past the fan test.

But That's Not All

The fan test isn't the only reason serous screenwriters need to master standard Hollywood format. Mark Twain was only joking when he said, "Anyone who can only think of one way to spell a word obviously lacks imagination." For the same reasons we need dictionaries and standardized spellings, we need standard formats. Not because we can't think of more than one way to lay out our vision on the page, but because we can think of too many.

The fact is that a standard format exists today in Hollywood and if we don't master it, if we rely only on our imaginations, we're bound to embarrass ourselves. Or appear ignorant. Or amateurs. Or confuse our readers because we haven't been clear. Or waste our time reinventing what already exists. A standard gives writers confidence that they're steering clear of all these dangers and frees them to think about more interesting things. Like their characters and stories.

Where Standard Format Came From

Pioneering filmmakers in Hollywood standardized screenplay format beginning as early as the 1920s. Look at a script from the silent era and you'll recognize the basic layout of the modern script page. With the addition of sound and dialogue, the format evolved. It evolved further when television arrived. But the truth is, the look of a script page in Hollywood has changed very little since the beginning.

During the 1960s and '70s, well before the appearance of the first PC and script writing software, screenplays and teleplays were being typed by large "mimeo" departments at studios and specialized script houses sprinkled around Hollywood. Probably the most important of these was Barbara's Place, a legendary script operation that turned out thousands of scripts over the years and whose typists and proofreaders became the industry's foremost guardians of standard script format.

By the early 1980s, that mantel passed to Warner Bros.' acclaimed script processing department, where numerous Barbara's Place stalwarts migrated with their exhaustive knowledge of the Hollywood script business. The studio provided what was then state-of-the-art computer technology, and soon laser printers the size of Winnebagos were churning out scripts around the clock at the astonishing rate of three pages per second for television series like *The Dukes of Hazzard*, *Designing Women*, *Murphy Brown*, and *ER*, and movies like *Lethal Weapon*, *Batman*, *Forrest Gump*, *Rain Man*, *Unforgiven*, *Three Kings*, and *Twister*.

I joined the Warner Bros. staff as a neophyte script proofreader in 1983. I remained for fourteen years. During my years at Warner Bros., I was privileged to learn from Barbara's Place veterans Les Miller, Tim Alfors, Vern Hedges, Val Evensen, Kathleen Hietala, and Gordon Barclay, a group unrivaled in their mastery of script formats. Together with a staff of skilled typists and supervisors assembled by the studio, we applied what we knew to countless thousands of scripts, not just for Warner Bros., but for literally every studio in Hollywood.

The knowledge I gained during my years at Warner Bros. serves me every day as a writer and a teacher of writers. That is the knowledge I first set out to record in this guide and which I dare to call complete and authoritative, not as a boast but as a tribute to the unassailable credentials of those who taught me.

Is "The Hollywood Standard" the Only Way?

Of course not. Good writers with long Hollywood careers will find details here with which to quibble. That's fine. The intent of this manual isn't to pick fights, condemn alternative approaches, or impose restrictions on rogue writers. The intent is simply to offer writers a set of time-honored guidelines that will help them produce scripts in a form that is highly readable, clear, and professional.

Using This Book

The Hollywood Standard is designed as a manual that every screenwriter, from neophyte to old pro, will want to keep within arm's reach. It is intended to be used as a reference, with the information organized for easy and immediate accessibility via the table of contents at the front of the book or the index at the back. You can spend just a short time reading through the new Quick Start Guide and learn the basics in well under an hour. Then, when you're in the throes of writing and need to see exactly how to set up a telescopic POV shot or review some fine point of handling camera direction, you can find the relevant guidelines and examples in a matter of seconds.

The Hollywood Standard doesn't cover story structure, character development, or dialogue. What it does cover is format and style, those components of a script that appear exclusively on the page and not the screen. Format is standard; style is personal and infinitely variable.

Throughout this manual, you'll find the rules of standard screenplay format. But you'll also find many examples of how to work within those rules to create your own crisp, professional, entertaining script-writing style.

Writing a great script is the most difficult human endeavor I've encountered. As you attempt it, I hope this book helps.

QUICK START GUIDE

What does a writer new to film and television writing need to know to start turning out pages that look like they were generated by a pro?

Ten things, more or less.

Here they are in brief. Each of these topics is treated in detail later in the book.

Thing #1: Use the right font

Use some form of Courier, Courier New, or Courier Final Draft.

```
Courier looks like this.  Without it, a script page
doesn't look like a script page and is doomed to be
recycled into a Starbucks cup, from which a more serious
screenwriter will sip while writing in Courier font.
```

Always use 12-point type. Don't cheat. People who stare at script pages for a living will know. And they'll turn your script into a coffee cup.

To read more about why 12-point Courier is the font of choice, see "Margins and fonts for single-camera film format."

Thing #2: Use the right margins

Script format relies on two sets of margins, those for the narrow strip of dialogue that runs down the center of the page, and those for everything else. Here is an example of how those two sets of margins appear on a typical script page:

```
INT. LIEUTENANT'S OFFICE

The new boss is a boxcar of a man named COFFEY.  He's
unpacking.  Lots of golf paraphernalia.  He looks up as
Will and Bobbie enter.  Will extends a hand.  He's got
the people skills Bobbie doesn't give a damn about.

                    WILL
          Detective Sampson and my partner
          Detective Loakes.  Welcome to
          Southern District, Lieutenant.
          I've heard good things.

Lt. Coffey shakes Will's hand but his gaze settles on
Bobbie.
```

```
                    LT. COFFEY
          Detective Loakes.  I've heard
          things about you.

                    BOBBIE
          What kind of things?

                    LT. COFFEY
          That you've got the best mind in
          the department.

                    BOBBIE
          Best mind in the department.  I
          like the sound of that.

     He unzips a leather golf bag, removes a five-iron.

                    LT. COFFEY
          And that you're difficult.

     Bobbie has no problem with eye contact now.

                    BOBBIE
          Well.  I think you'll find the
          one makes up for the other.

                                        CUT TO:
```

Notice that the names of characters over dialogue are indented. Notice also that the transition at the end of the short scene — "CUT TO:" — is tabbed far to the right side of the page. Precise margins for each of these elements can be found in the section, "Standard single-camera film format margins."

Because writing a script means shifting between these sets of margins many hundreds of times, writers need some efficient way to accomplish the margin shifts. This is where Final Draft comes in. Or Movie Magic Screenwriter. Or Celtx. Or Microsoft Word styles. With each of these software solutions, a writer can apply the appropriate margins with a simple keystroke or two. How to choose a method that works best for your budget and temperament is discussed in the chapter "Unleashing the Power of Script Typing Software."

Thing #3: Use the right paper, cover and brads

The rule here: Don't get creative. Stick with the basics.

- For paper, use plain vanilla 8.5-by-11-inch white, three-holed paper, the kind they sell for about $5 a ream at office supply stores.

- Bind the script with two brass brads (#5 brass round-head fasteners, manufactured by Acco work beautifully), one in the top hole and one in the bottom hole. Leave the center hole empty. For some Hollywood readers, a brad in the center hole constitutes a grave offense. No kidding.

- A cover is unnecessary. If the script is represented by an agent, the agency will put its own cover on the script before submitting it to buyers. Studios and production companies will put their own covers on scripts they own. Otherwise, present the script without a cover, or with a blank cover of 60-lb. card stock of any color.

Don't spiral bind a script. Don't put it in a folder or a three-ring binder. Don't put pictures on the cover. Don't include budgets, sketches, photos or casting suggestions. All of these will doom the script to return as a Starbucks cup. Keep it simple. Let the script speak for itself.

Thing #4: Put shot headings in the right places

Film and television scripts include headings at the beginning of each scene to indicate the location of the scene and the time of day it occurs. Sometimes these headings include additional information, like the type of shot to be used, or a notation that the scene takes place in slow motion, or underwater, or in the rain, or that it's a flashback or a dream sequence. These are variously called shot headings, scene headings or slug lines. They look like this:

```
EXT. MARTIAN CRATER - DAY

INT. ROADSIDE DINER - LADIES' ROOM - DAY

CLOSE SHOT - THUMBPRINT ON BROKEN BOTTLE

FLASHBACK - HOSPITAL NURSERY
```

Shot headings come in such great variety that the longest chapter in this book, "Shot Headings," is dedicated to covering the topic in detail.

Some writers use so many shot headings that they clutter their pages with unnecessary technical language, get in the way of telling their story, or give the off-putting impression that they're attempting to direct the film. Others use too few shot headings and their scripts read like stage plays stuck endlessly in one location.

In general, use shot headings as sparingly as possible, but do include them when necessary. Follow three basic rules to determine when a new shot heading is required.

Rule 1: A new shot heading is needed whenever the location changes.

Say a conversation between two fugitives is taking place inside a farmhouse, under the shot heading INT. FARMHOUSE - DAY, and then the fugitives step outside, onto the front porch. A new shot heading is needed to cover the exterior action: EXT. FARMHOUSE - FRONT PORCH - DAY.

Or let's say the action moves from INT. FARMHOUSE - BEDROOM to INT. FARMHOUSE - KITCHEN. Again, a new shot heading is needed.

And of course this applies when the location shift is even more dramatic, from INT. CRIPPLED APPOLO 13 COMMAND MODULE to INT. HOUSTON CONTROL.

Rule 2: A new shot heading is needed whenever the time changes.

This rule holds even if the location of the scene hasn't changed. Look at the following example.

```
INT. LIBRARY - DEAD OF NIGHT

Sylvia's eyelids are heavy as she sits over the dusty
book, forcing herself to keep reading.

She turns a page.  Seven hundred and thirty-two down.
Nine hundred and six to go.

Her eyes close.  Her head bobs.  She shakes herself back
to consciousness.

                         SYLVIA
            I'm good.  I'm awake.

                                             CUT TO:


INT. LIBRARY - MORNING

Light fills the room. Face down in the book, Sylvia
snores like a walrus with a head cold.
```

Rule 3: A new shot heading is needed when logic requires it.

An example will help make sense of this rule. Let's say a scene in a romantic comedy takes place at the female lead's school, inside her classroom. It opens like this:

```
INT. ROSIE'S KINDERGARTEN CLASSROOM - DAY

It's raining hard outside.  Rosie's at the classroom
door, helping arriving students fold dripping umbrellas
and pull their little feet out of rain boots.

She doesn't notice Allister at the front of the
classroom playing with the lid of the terrarium,
spinning it over his head like it's a helicopter rotor.

Rosie finishes with the umbrella.  Almost turns in time
to catch Allister making like a chopper.  But the door
```

```
blows open and rain flies in.  She pushes it closed.
Fumbles to get it latched.  Doesn't notice Allister, or:

TERRARIUM

Where the tarantula climbs onto the rim of the open
enclosure.  Teeters like an arachnid Baryshnikov.  And
drops into Rosie's open purse.
```

Now we want to go back to Rosie, to see her next action, but we can't do it directly, without first inserting a new shot heading, because Rosie can't be seen in the current shot of the terrarium. In this case, logic requires a new shot heading, either "INT. CLASSROOM," or "ROSIE" or "BACK TO SCENE," like this:

```
BACK TO SCENE

Rosie finally gets the door to stay closed and turns
toward the front of the classroom.

Allister has replaced the terrarium lid and has moved on
to dipping his fingers in a fish tank.

Rosie steers him toward his seat.
```

The same situation arises when POV, or point of view, shots are employed. Or close shots. Or any other time a writer indicates a shot that restricts our view to only a portion of a larger location. To get out of that restrictive shot, a new shot heading is usually needed.

Pay attention to the visual logic of your scenes. Add shot headings when logic demands it. But remember: Simpler is almost always better. Add shot headings only when you have a compelling storytelling reason to do so. For a more detailed discussion on this topic, see "How to decide when to create a new shot heading."

Thing #5: Put the contents of shot headings in the right order

Shot headings can consist of nothing more than a short description of a specific image:

```
BUG
```

At the other extreme, they can contain a great deal of complicated information, and sometimes become ungainly and bloated:

```
DREAM SEQUENCE - INT. MOUNT WEATHER PRESIDENTIAL BUNKER
- SITUATION ROOM - CLOSE SHOT - COMPUTER SCREEN - DAY
(SEPTEMBER 11, 2001) (GRAINY VIDEO FOOTAGE)
```

The same rule applies here: simpler is better. Include all necessary information and no more. Shot headings should only rarely wrap onto a second line, and a shot heading that fills three lines, like the example above, almost never occur. It is displayed here for illustration only, like a giant anaconda in a zoo.

Shot headings can include up to five categories of information. They may, however, contain only one piece of information, like the "BUG" example above. Arrange the necessary information in the following order:

1. *INT. or EXT.*, to indicate that the scene takes place in an interior or exterior location.

2. *The name of the location itself*, such as PRESIDENTIAL BUNKER or FARMHOUSE or SURFACE OF ELECTRON. The location can include multiple parts (e.g. PRESIDENTIAL BUNKER - SITUATION ROOM), and those parts should be listed from general to specific. Put the INT. or EXT. designation together with a location, and you get:

        EXT. HIGH SCHOOL FOOTBALL FIELD

        INT. ATTIC

        EXT. ROSE BOWL - PARKING LOT

3. *Type of shot*, for example EXTREME CLOSEUP or POV SHOT. Call for specific shots only when absolutely necessary.

4. *Subject of shot*. The subject of the shot can stand alone:

        ROSIE

Or it can be combined with a location:

        INT. MISSILE SILO - MARK IV ICBM

Or it can be combined with a type of shot:

        EXTREME CLOSEUP - GNAT'S EYEBALL

5. *Time of day*. The simplest and most common designations are DAY and NIGHT. More colorful or specific descriptions can also be used: MIDNIGHT, SUNSET or 3 AM:

        INT. OUTHOUSE - DAY

        EXT. WHITE HOUSE - GREENHOUSE - NIGHT

        INT. HOUSE OF BLUES - NOON

Shot headings are typed in all capital letters. They contain no ending punctuation, but EXT. and INT. are followed by periods, and all other elements are separated by a hyphen that is preceded and followed by a single space, as in the examples above.

Read much more about shot headings in the chapter titled "Shot headings."

Thing #6: Capitalize words in direction for the right three reasons

Scripts employ direction to introduce characters, describe settings, actions, sounds and camera movement, and to control pace. Because scripts are intended not only to be read but also to serve as technical documents that hundreds of filmmaking professionals will use to produce a film or television episode, some types of information is traditionally typed in all capital letters.

Capitalize the following three types of information when they occur in direction:

1. *The introduction of a speaking character.* The first time a speaking character appears on screen, capitalize that character's name:

```
The elevator doors slide open and JOSEPH MARTIN long-
jumps off.  Martin is 40s, in a grass-stained Steelers
jersey, cheap eyeglasses held together with silver duct
tape.  An odd bird.
```

2. *Sound effects and offscreen sounds.* Capitalize the thing making the sound and the sound it makes:

```
The MOTORIZED CONTRAPTION GROWLS as Martin tries to
start it.  After a promising SPUTTER, the ENGINE WHEEZES
and DIES.  Delighted for some reason by this turn of
events, Martin produces a STARTER'S PISTOL, raises it
over his head and FIRES TWICE.

From somewhere unseen, a CHILD CRIES, a COYOTE HOWLS and
a PHONE RINGS.
```

3. *Camera direction.* Capitalize the word "camera," any verb describing its movement, and any prepositions connected to that movement:

```
Prius leaps over the river of lava and runs for his
life, CAMERA MOVING WITH him THROUGH a twisting series
of dark passageways.
```

Put it all together and you get something like this:

```
HIGH ABOVE WORLD — DUSK

The CAMERA HOVERS, BROODING.  Down below, the dark earth
is shrouded in heavy fog.  The red towers of the Golden
Gate Bridge rise above the murk.  The rest of the city
lies hidden.

The CAMERA SINKS DOWN, DOWN, DOWN, INTO:
```

```
FOG - OLD PRIEST

hurries across a parking lot toward a Burger King.  He's
tall and thin like a scarecrow.  Or a modern-day Gandalf.
His name is PHINEAS GAGE.  He grips a folded newspaper.
A WIND is BLOWING.
```

Read more in "Capitalization in direction."

Thing #7: Keep your character names consistent over dialogue

The name of a speaking character appears over every bit of dialogue the character speaks:

```
                    BERTIE
         I can't stop lying!  Honest to
         Pete!
```

Don't make the mistake of calling the character Bertie over some of her speeches and Alberta or Frank's Daughter over others. Readers, casting directors and actors will pause to scratch their heads and wonder if all these names belong to the same character, or if there are actually multiple characters being referenced. For the sake of clarity, keep your character names consistent for the duration of the script.

Read more in "Character names over dialogue."

Thing #8: Control parenthetical character direction

Writers sometimes need to provide information about how a line is spoken, or business a character is performing while delivering a line. This information can appear in parenthetical character direction:

```
    The PHONE RINGS.  Bobbie picks it up.

                    BOBBIE
         This is Bobbie.
              (listens)
         I'll meet you there.
```

Observe the following guidelines for a professional presentation:

- Keep parenthetical character direction to a minimum. Most speeches should contain no parenthetical direction.

- Don't state the obvious. If context makes clear that a character is furious, don't write "(furiously)" in parenthetical direction.

- Make sure the direction pertains only to the speaking character.

8

- Indent parenthetical direction.

- Begin parenthetical direction with a lower-case letter, omitting "he" or "she."

- End parenthetical direction without a period.

- Don't end a speech with parenthetical direction.

- Keep it brief. Four lines is too long.

Read more in "Parenthetical character direction."

Thing #9: Say it shorter, say it faster

William Strunk and E. B. White, in their classic book *The Elements of Style*, implore writers to "omit needless words." Nowhere is that instruction more needful than in the field of writing for the screen. Readers who carry home backbreaking stacks of screenplays every weekend have no patience for paragraphs larded with needless words. Settings must be described in a handful of vivid words. Characters must be introduced in a single pithy sentence. Actions must be painted with extreme economy of language. Instead of this:

```
INT. BMW SHOWROOM

This BMW showroom is filled with shiny, sexy, over-
engineered Bavarian steel on wheels.  Eager salesmen
sell to upscale, self-important customers.  Right now,
though, all of these people have forgotten themselves, a
rare event indeed, to focus their attention on a woman
who is making a scene.  Her name is MARTHA LOAKES.
She's somewhere north of 40, south of 50, but looks like
she's older.  Her suit is dated.  Her makeup is bad.
She's wearing bathroom slippers.
```

Do this:

```
INT. BMW SHOWROOM

All that sexy Bavarian steel.  Salesmen and upscale
customers focus on MARTHA LOAKES, 50s, weathered,
wearing a dated suit, bad makeup and bathroom slippers.
```

With every word keep moving forward, revealing character, unveiling mysteries, in succinct, powerful, lean prose.

Thing #10: Break pages in the right places

Final Draft, Movie Magic Screenwriter, and Celtx can help here. Ultimately, though, the writer bears responsibility for observing these reasonable and time-honored conventions.

Whenever possible, break pages between paragraphs of direction or between speeches:

                         MARTHA
               I tried to call your father. I
               couldn't reach him anywhere.

                         BOBBIE
               You try the cemetery?

          ---------------Page break---------------

                                                  11.

          Too much truth. Martha shouts:

                         MARTHA
               <u>I'M NOT LEAVING HERE WITHOUT MY</u>
               <u>CAR</u>.

          Everyone stares. Bobbie stares right back, caught with
          her self-assurance down around her ankles.

                         BOBBIE
               This is a mentally ill person.
               Do you mind?

If a paragraph of direction or speech is too long to fit on a page, move it to the next page. However, if moving the entire paragraph or speech to the next page will leave an excessively short page, the direction or dialogue must be broken between pages. Follow these guidelines:

When breaking dialogue or direction, always break at the end of a sentence, not in the middle.

          INT. BMW SHOWROOM

          All that sexy Bavarian steel.

          ---------------Page break---------------

                                                  42.

          Salesmen and upscale customers focus on MARTHA LOAKES,
          50s, weathered, wearing a dated suit, bad makeup and
          bathroom slippers.

When breaking dialogue, add (MORE) at the bottom of the page and (CONT'D) at the top of the following page, beside the character name. Break before parenthetical character direction, not after.

```
                    WILL
          The summer Pam was dying, I
          couldn't string two coherent
          thoughts together to save my
          life.  You covered for me,
          Bobbie.  Hell, sometimes I think
          you're still covering for me.
                    (MORE)

    ---------------Page break---------------
```
                                                           14.

```
                    WILL (CONT'D)
                (beat)
          Now it's my turn.  Let me share
          the load on this one.  We'll find
          the answers.
```

Don't break a page immediately after a shot heading. Instead, carry the shot heading to the top of the next page.

Don't break a page immediately before a transition, such as a CUT TO:. Instead, keep the transition on the same page with the scene that precedes it.

For detailed instructions about breaking pages, see the following sections:

- "Breaking a page after a shot heading"
- "Breaking a page in the middle of direction"
- "Breaking a page in the middle of dialogue"
- "Breaking a page at a transition"
- "Act breaks"

Now get started writing. Use the table of contents at the front of this book or the index at the back to find more detailed information and examples whenever questions arise. Or, to learn more of the fundamentals quickly, read the next chapter, "Avoiding a Dozen Deadly Formatting Mistakes."

AVOIDING A DOZEN DEADLY FORMATTING MISTAKES

As creative as we like to think we are, we writers repeat the same rookie mistakes again and again. Here are a dozen of the most common and glaring errors, culled from the pages of discarded scripts on their way to the recycling factory.

Deadly mistake #1: Getting cute with pictures and fonts on the title page

The temptation is great. The photograph of the grizzled fur trapper and his three-legged puppy would look marvelous on the title page, especially with the title set in 36-point Sasquatch and printed in leather-colored ink.

Don't do it.

Keep the title page simple and clean. Title. Writer's name. Contact information. All in 12-point Courier font. White paper. Black ink.

The title page won't sell the script. But it can make a disastrous first impression.

Read more in "Title pages."

Deadly mistake #2: Submitting faded print or wrinkled pages

Don't sabotage your enormous creative effort by submitting a script printed in disappearing ink or stained with the drippings of last night's Hot Pocket.

Competition in this game is intense. Neatness counts.

Deadly mistake #3: Cheating the margins and thinking you're going to get away with it

People who make movies take their margins seriously.

Seriously.

All of us have more words we'd like to pack into those few pages we're allowed. Fuller descriptions. A longer chase sequence. Another conversation between that trapper and his dog. All writers face the battle of the bulge.

When we've written too many words, the solution is not to cheat the margins. The solution is to cut words. It hurts. You're a writer. Be tough. Cut.

When we refuse to cut, when we instead alter the margins so that we can pack our pages with too many words, bad things happen. Pages turn more slowly. Reading our scripts becomes a chore. Readers notice. They tune out. They skim. They pass.

Don't cheat.

Deadly mistake #4: Neglecting to search and destroy

Imagine opening a screenplay and reading these first glorious lines:

```
FAED INN:

FEMININ HADNS

grip black steal.  Expertly disassembal a Glock nine-
millameter.  Click.  Click.  Clic.k

The peaces of the gun are spred across a woman's vanity.
Her hands swiftly clean each peas of the weapon.  Longue
fingers, Soft skin

The gun goes back to4ether fast.  Snap.  Sanp.  Snap.
```

While these words may introduce the most compelling story ever imagined, this screenplay will never go in front of the cameras because no one will read it.

Why should they? The writer obviously hasn't.

Take the time to read what you've written. Not what you think you've written, but the actual letters and punctuation marks you've put on the page. That means reading slowly. Meticulously. Fixing the missing punctuation. The creative spelling. The inadvertent omissions. The "who's" where you meant "whose." The bit of dialogue that somehow got formatted as direction. The typos.

That stuff.

Don't be too proud to ask for help. Not all great writers are great spellers. Or proofreaders. But they want their scripts to be taken seriously, so they find a way to purge their pages of mistakes.

Error-free pages communicate respect for yourself, your craft and your readers. Search out those errors. Destroy them.

Deadly mistake #5: Overusing shot headings

Film and television writers can create in the imaginations of their readers something very close to the experience of actually watching a story unfold on the screen. But pages peppered with medium shots, two shots, wide shots and tracking shots intrude on that illusion. Further, they

14

suggest that the writer doesn't understand the line between the work of the writer and that of the director. Or is new to the game and simply doesn't know any better.

Use shot headings only when you have a compelling reason to do so. Otherwise, get out of the way and let the story unfold.

Read much more about this in "How to decide when to create a new shot heading."

Deadly mistake #6: Underusing shot headings

Screenplays and teleplays do require shot headings, and writers should include them when they are needed. Consider the following:

```
FADE IN:

A supernova bursts in a colossal explosion of white
heat.

A shockwave of hypercompressed sound and light rumbles
across the universe.  Directly in the path of the deadly
cosmic tsunami:

A familiar blue-green planet, third out from its sun.

Somewhere on Earth, a young girl wakes in her bed.
Innocent.  Unaware of the onrushing calamity.
```

This reads more like a short story than a screenplay, and demonstrates that the writer doesn't know his craft. Instead, format the sequence something like this:

```
FADE IN:

DEEP SPACE

A supernova bursts in a colossal explosion of white
heat.

A shockwave of hypercompressed sound and light rumbles
across the universe.  Directly in the path of the deadly
cosmic tsunami:


FAMILIAR BLUE-GREEN PLANET

Third out from its sun.
```

15

```
INT. CHILD'S BEDROOM - NIGHT

Somewhere on Earth, a young girl wakes in her bed.
Innocent.  Unaware of the onrushing calamity.
```

New shot headings are needed whenever the location changes, or whenever there is a jump in time. To read more about when shot headings are required, see "How to decide when to create a new shot heading."

Deadly mistake #7: Creating shot headings that are unnecessarily long

Short shot headings read more quickly than long ones. Building shot headings that include only the relevant information has the added benefit of focusing the reader's attention where it belongs. Take the following example.

```
EXT. CEMETERY - DAY

Grantham reaches between the broken bricks and pulls
out:


EXT. CEMETERY - CLOSE SHOT - RUSTED HANDGUN - DAY

The barrel is bent almost in half.
```

The vital information — that Grantham has produced a handgun — is buried inside an unnecessarily detailed shot heading. The EXT. CEMETERY location has already been established, as has the time of day, so those items don't need to be repeated within the context of a scene that is plainly continuous. Besides distracting from the one crucial piece of information in the shot heading, the rusted handgun, repeating the location and time of day makes the reader pause and wonder if a new scene has begun. And the type of shot, a close shot, is implicit in the words "rusted handgun." When a reader sees a relatively small object as the subject of a shot heading, what else does she imagine but a rusted handgun viewed from close range? Instead, write the sequence like this:

```
EXT. CEMETERY - DAY

Grantham reaches between the broken bricks and pulls
out:


RUSTED HANDGUN

The barrel is bent almost in half.
```

Deadly mistake #8: Mishandling parenthetical direction

Pay attention to the way standard format handles parenthetical character direction, which should begin on a new line, with a lower-case letter, and no ending period, like this:

```
                    CHARLOTTE
          Lieutenant, order your men to dig
          a trench there --
                    (points at cave
                     entrance)
          -- and another over there.

     She indicates the armory.
```

Don't embed parenthetical direction on the same line as dialogue:

```
                    CHARLOTTE
          Lieutenant, order your men to dig
          a trench there -- (points at cave
          entrance) -- and another over
          there.
```

And don't finish a speech with parenthetical direction dangling off the end (unless you're writing for animation):

```
                    CHARLOTTE
          Lieutenant, order your men to dig
          a trench there --
                    (points at cave
                     entrance)
          -- and another over there.
                    (indicates the armory)
```

Learn more by reading "Parenthetical character direction."

Deadly mistake #9: Using too many words

Screenplays and teleplays demand vivid, economical writing. Every word must contribute to the script's characters, visuals, action or attitude. All words that fail to contribute must be cut. Nearly every writer faces the need to slash surplus adverbs, adjectives, even entire sentences and paragraphs. Writers who refuse to cut test the patience of overworked readers and will almost certainly fail that test. After writing, cut, cut, cut, then cut some more. Give yourself a chance to make a strong professional impression as a writer who makes every word count.

Deadly mistake #10: Using up all the oxygen

Seasoned writers ensure that their pages contain abundant white space — that portion of the page without any words. White space allows script pages to breathe. A page with ample breathing room looks easy to read. Lack of this essential white space takes a strong psychological toll on the reader, who looks at a page dense with text and groans like a traveler forced to trudge through heavy mud.

Create white space by breaking long paragraphs into shorter ones. Break up long speeches with short bits of direction, or with dialogue from other characters.

Learn how to create white space in action sequences by reading the section "Add shot headings to break up long passages of action and lend a sense of increased tempo."

Deadly mistake #11: Writing too many pages

Writers who write excessively long scripts don't get read. The preferred length for a feature screenplay is 100 to 110 pages, with some comedies and animated features coming in even shorter. A script of this length is fast to read and manageable to shoot. A script that weighs in at 120 pages, once considered an appropriate length, is now viewed as too long. A script of 135 pages likely won't even be read.

For writers in television, acceptable page counts vary from show to show. Before writing a spec (i.e "speculative") episode of an existing television series, obtain a sample script and match the page count as closely as possible.

Deadly mistake #12: Slipping into the past tense

Descriptive passages in scripts, also called direction, are written in present tense prose, like this:

```
EXT. DOWNTOWN SAN FRANCISCO - MORNING

A red Jeep rolls along Market Street.  Turns south on
Eighth. FOLLOW as it joins a line of cars turning into
the San Francisco Hall of Justice.  Catch a glimpse of
Bobbie at the wheel.


INT. HALL OF JUSTICE

Bobbie plunges into the chaos of the 7 AM shift change
in this big city detectives' bureau.  She pulls case
files from her inbox and threads her way through the
chitchat with absolute self-assurance.  No pleasantries,
no eye contact.  Like she's the only one in the room.
Will steps into her path.
```

Scribes more accustomed to writing short stories or novels sometimes slip into past tense. Instead of "Will steps into her path," they inadvertently write, "Will stepped into her path." It's an understandable mistake, but it's also a tip-off that the writer is new to film and television and need not be taken seriously. The goal, of course, is to be taken as seriously as a third Coen brother, so search out this error during proofreading and destroy it.

Writers who train themselves to avoid these dozen deadly mistakes will give their scripts a chance for serious consideration in today's environment of extreme competition for the attention of readers who can help them bring their stories to the screen.

FAQs about Ten Things and Deadly Mistakes

No one has really, um, died from making one of these mistakes... have they?

No.

You say that 120 pages is too long for a script, but I see movies all the time that are longer than two hours. If it's a page a minute, how long are those scripts, and how come mine can't be that long?

Yes, we see movies all the time that come in at well over two hours. But it's a safe bet that those movies didn't begin as 180 page spec scripts. *Titanic*? *Lord of the Rings*? Not specs. Those deals were in place with studios before a single page was written. Different world, different rules. Unless you're James Cameron or Peter Jackson and his brilliant co-writers, keep it under 110 pages and you'll give yourself a shot at getting read by someone who doesn't start out resenting you.

I heard a successful writer say that scripts should always have covers, and that those covers should always be that vibrant shade of electric blue. He says every script he puts that cover on sells.

And some of baseball's hottest hitters credit the lucky rabbit's foot in their pocket or the fact that they never shave after August 15. I think there's probably something else at play. Like talent and hard work. In any case, use the blue cover if you want to. It won't hurt anything. But a writer who sells regularly is doing more right than choosing a jazzy script cover.

I heard that same successful writer say that you shouldn't use any commas in your script. He doesn't, and he sells everything he writes.

See "Lucky rabbit's foot" and "No shaving after August 15." I don't doubt that this writer sells a bunch of scripts, but it's not due to the lack of commas in his work. Many equally successful writers use commas like the rest of the English-speaking world, to no ill effect.

I'm trying to follow your margins in Microsoft Word, but I can't get as many lines on the page as you recommend. Is there a trick that will help me?

Yes. In Word, select Format, Paragraph, Line Spacing, then select Exactly and 12 pt. Word will then allow exactly 12 points per line, the historic standard for screenplays in Hollywood, and you'll be able to fit the correct number of lines on each page.

SPEC SCRIPTS VS. PRODUCTION DRAFTS

What's the difference?

This question needlessly vexes many writers. Some have been told that spec scripts look dramatically different from production drafts.

They don't. They shouldn't. Except in a tiny handful of specific ways.

First a couple of definitions. A *spec script* is one that is written speculatively, rather than on assignment for an employer such as a production company, network or studio, in hopes of later selling it to someone who will shoot it. A *production draft* is a script that has reached active preproduction or production.

The primary audience for a spec script is the buyer. Or, more precisely, the reader who works for the buyer, either a producer or a network or studio executive. Agents, directors and actors are also primary readers of spec scripts. Spec scripts should be written with this fact firmly in mind. The spec script is meant to be read, and should be written in such a way that it is a delight to the reader's eye. That means as few shot headings as possible, simple shot headings, economical direction, and only rare parenthetical character direction, camera direction, sound direction and scene transitions.

But, except for the fact that a production draft is being read by many more people in a greater variety of disciplines because it is being shot, *all of these things are equally true of the production draft.* The production draft should contain a minimum of shot headings, each as simply worded as possible. It should be written economically. Parenthetical character direction, camera direction, sound direction and scene transitions should be kept to a minimum. For all of the same reasons.

In fact, production drafts are rarely anything other than spec scripts that have been purchased, rewritten again and again, polished, rewritten some more, and, here's the big, stinkin' difference, have had scene numbers added beside each shot heading. At no time does the writer sit down and type additional shot headings or transitions or anything else into the script to turn it into a production draft. In fact, until cameras start rolling, no one knows which draft will be the final, or production, draft.

During production, individual shots — wide shots, medium shots, two shots, closeups, and so on — are hand-written into the script by the script supervisor. Dialogue is often improvised or rewritten on set as it is being shot. These changes don't get typed into the script.

Script changes are made, it is true, during shooting, for scenes yet to be shot. As pages are revised during preproduction and production, those pages are printed on colored paper, page numbers are "locked" (read all about the changes a script undergoes during production in the chapter "The Evolution of a Script from First Draft to Production Draft"), and asterisks are typed in the right margin to indicate the locations of changes. Writers don't need to worry about this stage of a script's development. Production offices handle these changes in feature film production. Writers' assistants handle them in television production.

The bottom line for writers is this. Put your film or television story on the page in a way that is easy to read and visualize. Keep all technical references to camera angles, sound effects and scene transitions as spare and unobtrusive as possible. Serve the imagination of your reader. But don't be afraid to call for a camera move if you have a compelling reason to do so. Or to indicate important sounds. Or to add essential character direction parenthetically in dialogue. These are all tools of the script writer. Don't cheat yourself out of using them because someone has made an absolute pronouncement against them. Professional writers use every tool in the box. They use them smartly. They use them for good reasons and to exquisite effect. They use them with restraint. But use them they do.

SINGLE-CAMERA FILM FORMAT

This is the classic screenplay format developed over decades of Hollywood history. It is used for productions filmed principally with one camera:

- theatrical feature films
- hour-long television drama
- much half-hour television comedy (with the exception of traditional multi-camera sitcoms shot in the style of shows like *Two and a Half Men*)
- long-form television, including made-for-television movies and miniseries

The four building blocks of single-camera film format

Despite their potential to map out film and television of soaring imagination, beauty and complexity, screenplays and teleplays consist of only four basic format elements: **shot headings**, **direction**, **dialogue**, and **transitions**.

Shot headings begin each new scene or shot. They may give general information about a scene's location and the time of day the scene takes place:

```
INT. PENTAGON - FIFTH FLOOR CORRIDOR - DAY
```

Or they may give information about the type and subject of a specific shot:

```
EXTREME CLOSEUP - WANDA'S TRIGGER FINGER
```

Shot headings are most often followed by *direction*, passages that describe what is being seen and heard within the shot or scene:

```
Micah crawls under the fence, the barbed wire snagging
his tattered jumpsuit.  The beam of a searchlight passes
and he presses himself into the ground, desperate to
make himself invisible.
```

Dialogue consists of the name of the character who is speaking, the actual words that are spoken, and any parenthetical character direction related to the dialogue:

```
                    MIMI
        That just figures, don't it?
              (smacks steering
               wheel)
        I go and steal me a car without
        no gas.
```

Transitions sometimes appear at the end of scenes and indicate how one scene links to the next:

DISSOLVE TO:

See *Appendix A* for sample script pages in single-camera film format.

Margins and fonts for single-camera film format

Standard format dictates that scripts always use a *fixed-pitch font*, such as Courier or Courier New, and adhere to *standard margins*. A fixed-pitch font (as opposed to a proportionally spaced font like the one used in this paragraph) is one in which every letter occupies the same amount of horizontal space on the line, regardless of whether it is a lower case i or a capital M. Fonts used for typing scripts are 10 pitch, meaning there are 10 characters per horizontal inch, and 12 points, which allows six lines of type per vertical inch. Twelve-point Courier or Courier New fit the bill and are the fonts most often used in scripts. Used in combination with a fixed-pitch font, standard margins result in script pages with a relatively uniform amount of content per page.

Why is this important?

Over the years, a rule of thumb developed among filmmakers that one script page translated, on average, into one minute of finished film. Production cost estimates also came to be based in part on the number of pages in a script or scene. So did the amount of time allotted for filming scenes. Television writers knew that if they wrote roughly 60 pages, they had the right amount of material for a one-hour show. Feature writers knew that a 120-page screenplay represented a film of about two hours. And despite any number of quibbles one may have with these formulas (scripts for the brooding one-hour series *China Beach* often ran as few as 50 pages while scripts for the hyperkinetic *ER*, also an hour long, sometimes stretched up to 70 pages), they are indelibly part of the day-in and day-out workings of Hollywood even today. Production schedules are set based on the number of pages to be shot per day. Writers make decisions about whether or not to cut a scene based on their script's page count. An accurate page count is taken so seriously in Hollywood that senior executives at Warner Bros. once threatened to disband their own script processing department when they suspected its staff had compromised standard script margins on one critical draft of a feature film script. Altering a script's font or margins or even paper size from the standard changes the amount of material that fits on a page and thereby upsets all the calculations based on script page counts. It also changes the appearance of the page in ways that can instantly brand a script as unprofessional. Writers do so at their own peril.

A script page typed with standard margins looks like this:

[9]14.

[8]21   [2]EXT. BATTLEFIELD - DAWN   [8]21

[3]The sun rises crimson over the fallen soldiers. Ragged
children move among the dead, searching for survivors.
Or a serviceable pair of boots.

                    [5]UNION CAPTAIN
          [4]You younguns, git!
              [6](turning to his
                  men)
          Ever'body knows his job. Let's
          git to it!

The men start reluctantly across the field.

                                        [7]CUT TO:

22   EXT. GRANT'S HEADQUARTERS - NIGHT   22

A fire burns outside a dirty canvas tent. Officers
mill. Everyone seems to be waiting for something to
happen.

Standard single-camera film format margins

Standard single-camera film format margins are as follows:

1.   **Paper** is 3-hole punched 8.5" x 11" white 20 lb. bond.

2.   **Shot headings**:
          Left margin is 1.7"
          Right margin is 1.1"
          Line length is 57 characters

3.   **Direction**:
          Left margin is 1.7"
          Right margin is 1.1"
          Line length is 57 characters

4. **Dialogue**:
>   Left margin is 2.7"
>   Right margin is 2.4"
>   Line length is 34 characters

5. **Character name over dialogue**:
>   Left margin is 4.1"
>> **Note that the character name over dialogue is not centered.** It begins at the same fixed point (4.1" from the left edge of the page) no matter how long it is.

6. **Parenthetical character direction**:
>   Left margin is 3.4"
>   Right margin is 3.1"
>   Line length is 19 characters

7. **Scene transitions**:
>   Left margin is 6.0"

8. **Scene numbers**:
>   Left scene number goes 1.0" from the left edge of the page
>   Right scene number goes 7.4" from the left edge of the page
>> **Note that scene numbers should not be added by the writer.** Scene numbers are added by the production office when a script goes into active preproduction.

9. **Page numbers**:
>   Go at 7.2", .5" below the top edge of the page.

10. **Font**:
>   Courier or Courier New 12 point (or equivalent fixed-pitch serif font)

11. **Page length**:
>   A maximum of 57 lines (which allows for .5" margin at the top and 1" margin at the bottom of each page)
>
>   These 57 lines include one line at the top of each page for the page number, followed by a blank line and the text of the script.

See page 28 for a sample with standard single-camera film margins. Use it as a template against which to compare the margins of your own pages.

Are script pages printed on one side of the page or two?

In an effort to save paper, some studios have experimented with double-sided script printing and some literary agencies routinely copy scripts on both sides of the page. Nevertheless, the longstanding practice in Hollywood has been to print scripts only on one side of the page. This makes reading the script far easier and provides room for the abundant notes that are regularly written on script pages. In addition, once a project approaches production, single-sided printing is an absolute necessity to make possible the replacement of individual script pages with colored revision pages.

                         BOBBIE
          There are some details missing
          from his statement to the other
          detectives. We need him to fill
          in the blanks.

                    FATHER PETROCELLI
                  (studies the cops)
          You understand the bullet passed
          through his brain. Father Gage
          is not the man he was.

INT. UPSTAIRS HALLWAY

Father Petrocelli leads Bobbie and Will down a dim
passage. At the far end he knocks softly on a door,
then turns the knob and pushes it open.

                    FATHER PETROCELLI
          If you need me, I'll be close by.

INT. FATHER GAGE'S QUARTERS

A bed. A desk. A lamp. Nothing more. Father Gage
bends over the desk, his head wrapped in gauze, a pencil
in his hand, scratching out a manuscript. He finishes
the page and places it atop a stack on the floor. There
are other stacks. He has written hundreds of pages. He
starts another.

                         WILL
          Father, we're sorry to bother
          you. We're detectives from San
          Francisco PD. We need to ask you
          a few questions.

Gage doesn't look up.

                         WILL
          What are you writing?

                    FATHER GAGE
          A book.

                         WILL
          What about?

Gage throws down the pencil, pushes back from the desk
and rises to his full, towering height.

                    FATHER GAGE
          Are you a believer?

Also called *scene headings* and *slug lines*, shot headings can provide a wide variety of information about a given scene or shot. **They are always typed in capital letters.** They can be short and sweet:

```
BOB
```

Or long and complicated:

```
EXT. WHITE HOUSE - SOUTH LAWN - CLOSE ON CNN
CORRESPONDENT - SUNSET (MARCH 15, 1999)
```

An important caveat

This chapter illustrates the proper use of a great variety of shot headings, from reverse angles to underwater shots. If you have a compelling reason to use one of these shots, this section shows how to do so in a professional, time-honored manner. However, the fundamental rule stands: Use as few shot headings as possible, and keep them as simple as you can. Most scenes require only a *master shot heading*, that is a single slug line to establish the location and time of day, like this:

```
EXT. CENTRAL PARK - DAY
```

The action and dialogue of the scene can then flow without further interruption, and without any additional shots being specified. Effective writers avoid overloading their pages with unnecessary, or overcomplicated, shot headings.

Sometimes, though, additional information must be included in a shot heading, or additional shot headings are needed to tell the story clearly and forcefully. This chapter explains how to determine when to use a new shot heading, which information should be included, and how that information should be arranged.

The five parts of a shot heading

Shot headings consist of up to five basic categories of information: 1) *interior* or *exterior*; 2) *location*; 3) *type of shot*; 4) *subject of shot*; and 5) *time of day*.

Interior or Exterior

A shot heading may begin with the abbreviation EXT., which stands for exterior. It tells us the scene takes place outdoors, a critical piece of information for anyone involved in production since most exterior scenes are shot outdoors rather than inside a sound stage.

The abbreviation INT. stands for interior and tells us the scene takes place indoors. Interior scenes are often shot on a stage.

INT. and EXT. are always capitalized and followed by a period and a single space, like this:

```
INT. SPACE STATION
```

Not:

```
INT.  SPACE STATION

Int. Space Station

INT: SPACE STATION

INT SPACE STATION

INT - SPACE STATION
```

Once in a while, a scene takes place both inside and outside. Let's say Molly, a sweet, ordinary girl, is locked in a battle with a wolverine while she's driving her Ferrari along the Hollywood Freeway and will be climbing onto the hood of her car during the shot. There are a couple of ways to set that up:

```
EXT. HOLLYWOOD FREEWAY/INT. MOLLY'S FERRARI - DAY

Steering with her bare feet, Molly hoists herself
through the open window, wildly swinging her purse at
the rabid wolverine.
```

Or:

```
EXT./INT. MOLLY'S FERRARI - DAY

Racing along the Hollywood Freeway.  Steering with her
feet, Molly hoists herself through the open window,
wildly swinging her purse at the rabid wolverine.
```

Note that EXT./INT. contains a period after each abbreviation.

Sometimes writers are unsure whether a scene should be designated INT. or EXT. Our hero may have just climbed out of his car — after driving it into his garage. EXT. CAR isn't the correct designation because the scene is actually taking place inside the garage. Correct shot headings in this case include INT. GARAGE - OUTSIDE CAR or simply INT. GARAGE.

What if a scene is taking place inside an open-air stadium? It's still outdoors, so it's EXT.:

```
EXT. FENWAY PARK - UPPER DECK
```

Not:

```
INT. FENWAY PARK - UPPER DECK
```

Just think "INT. for indoors" and "EXT. for outdoors" and you'll know what to do.

An important rule: **If you use a designation of INT. or EXT., you must always follow it immediately with a location:**

```
EXT. GOLDEN GATE PARK - JACK
```

Not:

```
EXT. JACK IN GOLDEN GATE PARK

EXT. JACK

EXT. DAY

EXT. WIDE SHOT - JACK
```

Location

Location tells us where the scene takes place:

```
EXT. SURFACE OF MOON - TRANQUILITY BASE

INT. MUSTANG - TRUNK SPACE

INT. HONOLULU HILTON - PRESIDENTIAL SUITE - BATHROOM

EXT. FRED'S BACK YARD
```

An important rule: **A shot heading may contain just one location element or several, but those elements are always listed in order** *from general to specific,* **with each element separated by a hyphen (single space, hyphen, single space), like so:**

```
EXT. LOS ANGELES - DOWNTOWN - BONAVENTURE HOTEL -
LOADING DOCK
```

31

Not:

        INT. DRESSING ROOM - STARLET'S TRAILER
           (This one gets it backward, starting specific then going general.)

        CORN FIELD -- FARM -- IOWA
           (Again, the order is backward, and the hyphens are wrong.)

        EXT. MANHATTAN STREET. SCENE OF CAR ACCIDENT. SOHO.
           (The order here is scrambled and the hyphens have been replaced by periods.)

When an interior location includes a city name, put the city name in parentheses after the main location entry:

        INT. RAMSHACKLE WAREHOUSE (HONOLULU) - DAY

        INT. HOTEL ADLON (BERLIN) - 7TH FLOOR GUEST ROOM - NIGHT

Type of shot

Sometimes a writer wants to indicate a specific type of shot. There are many: establishing shots, wide shots, close shots, tracking shots, extreme closeups, insert shots, underwater shots, POV shots and more. How frequently new shot headings should be inserted is a matter of much controversy and confusion. For now, we will list each type of shot and how each is properly formatted. Later, we will discuss some guidelines both practical and stylistic that will help writers decide when new shots should and should not be used.

Closeup

A *closeup shot* indicates that the camera is focusing closely on a subject. Close shots can be set up in a variety of ways. Each of the following is correct:

        CLOSE - RUDOLPH'S NOSE

        CLOSE SHOT - RUDOLPH'S NOSE

        CLOSEUP - RUDOLPH'S NOSE

        CLOSE ON RUDOLPH'S NOSE

        CLOSE ANGLE ON RUDOLPH'S NOSE

Note that CLOSE, CLOSE SHOT and CLOSEUP are all followed by a hyphen, while CLOSE ON and CLOSE ANGLE ON are not. Note also that CLOSEUP is one word, not two.

Extreme closeup

A variant of the closeup is the *extreme closeup*:

```
EXTREME CLOSEUP - IRIS OF WILLIAM'S LEFT EYE
```

Insert shot

An *insert shot* is a special kind of closeup featuring a prop to show some important detail. Often an insert shot focuses on the written text of a sign, book or note:

```
JOHN

rips the envelope and pulls out a birthday card.  He
opens it.

INSERT - CARD

Words scrawled in burgundy lipstick: "ENJOY YOUR
BIRTHDAY.  IT'S YOUR LAST."

BACK TO SCENE

John reacts with alarm.  He takes a closer look at the
envelope.
```

Note that after an insert shot, a new shot heading is necessary to bring us back into the main action. *Back to scene* is a useful, generic shot heading to accomplish that.

Wide shot

A *wide shot* moves the camera away from the subject and takes in a swath of scenery. Wide shots can be set up in any of the following ways:

```
WIDE - RACETRACK AND EMPTY STANDS

WIDE SHOT - RACETRACK AND EMPTY STANDS

WIDE ANGLE - RACETRACK AND EMPTY STANDS

WIDE ON RACETRACK AND EMPTY STANDS

WIDE ANGLE ON RACETRACK AND EMPTY STANDS
```

As before, when the preposition "on" is used, a hyphen is not.

33

Medium shot

Between the wide shot and the closeup is the *medium shot*, abbreviated MED. SHOT. Its subject is always one or more characters and it comes in only one flavor, like so:

```
MED. SHOT - JACK AND ROSE
```

Not:

```
MEDIUM SHOT - JACK AND ROSE
```
(Don't spell out MEDIUM.)

```
MED. SHOT ON JACK AND ROSE
```
(Don't use the preposition ON)

```
MED. - JACK AND ROSE
```
(Don't omit the word SHOT)

An important reminder: Just because a shot type exists doesn't mean it's a good idea to use it, for many of the same reasons you shouldn't use every word in the dictionary in casual conversation. It's difficult to imagine a scenario in which a writer would need to specify a medium shot, two shot or three shot. But should that occasion arise, this is how it's done.

Two and three shot

A *two shot* is framed to feature two characters. A *three shot* features three characters:

```
TWO SHOT - BRUTUS AND CAESAR

THREE SHOT - MANNY, MOE AND JACK
```

Not:

```
BRUTUS AND CAESAR - TWO SHOT
```
(The subject of the shot should *follow* the type of shot.)

```
THREE SHOT OF MANNY, MOE AND JACK
```
(Use a hyphen instead of the word OF)

Establishing shot

An *establishing shot* is used to show the exterior of a location, usually a building of some kind, inside which the next scene will take place. **In a true establishing shot, no action specific to the story takes place and no recognizable characters appear.** It is simply a shot that establishes the identity of the building we are about to go inside and the time of day. It can be set up like this:

```
EXT. BERTIE'S BREWHOUSE - ESTABLISHING SHOT - DAY

The parking lot is empty.

                                        CUT TO:

INT. BERTIE'S BREWHOUSE

Bertie mops the floor.
```

The following are also correct:

```
EXT. BERTIE'S BREWHOUSE - DAY

ESTABLISHING.  The parking lot is empty.

EXT. BERTIE'S BREWHOUSE - ESTABLISHING - DAY

EXT. BERTIE'S BREWHOUSE - DAY (ESTABLISHING)

EXT. BERTIE'S BREWHOUSE - TO ESTABLISH - DAY
```

Not:

```
EXT. BERTIE'S BREWHOUSE - ESTABLISHING - DAY

Bertie trudges outside and dumps a bucket of dirty
water.
```
(If you have specific characters or action in the shot like we do here, it is not an establishing shot. Just drop the word "establishing" and you've got a perfectly formatted scene.)

Tracking and moving shot

In a *tracking shot*, the camera moves with the action. Closely related is the *moving shot*. All of the following are correct:

```
TRACKING SHOT - MAN OF WAR

gallops down the back stretch, kicking up heavy clumps
of mud.

TRACKING SHOT

Man of War gallops down the back stretch, kicking up
heavy clumps of mud.
```

```
INT. MUSTANG CONVERTIBLE - MOVING - DAY

EXT. FIFTH AVENUE - MOVING SHOT - GRETA AND CURTIS

MOVING WITH PARADE FLOAT

TRACKING MAN OF WAR
```

Not:

```
MOVING WITH - PARADE FLOAT
```
    (The preposition WITH eliminates the need for the hyphen.)

```
TRACKING - MAN OF WAR
```
    (Either add the word SHOT after TRACKING or eliminate the hyphen.)

Aerial shot

An *aerial shot* is photographed from the air:

```
AERIAL SHOT - BEACHES OF NORMANDY

EXT. BEACHES OF NORMANDY - AERIAL SHOT - D-DAY
```

Underwater shot

An *underwater shot* can be formatted in a couple of different ways:

```
INT. GIANT AQUARIUM - MOVING WITH SHARK (UNDERWATER) -
DAY

UNDERWATER SHOT - DECK OF SUNKEN FREIGHTER
```

New angle

Sometimes a writer may want to indicate a *new angle* within an existing scene without specifying exactly what sort of angle it is. These shot headings may be formatted as follows:

```
NEW ANGLE

NEW ANGLE - BALL FIELD

ANGLE - PANTING GOLDEN RETRIEVER

ANGLE ON SOPHIA
```

Sometimes ANGLE ON is shortened to just ON:

```
EXT. VENICE BEACH - ON SOPHIA - DAY

ON MIKE'S CLENCHED FIST
```

Note that ANGLE or NEW ANGLE should be used only within an existing scene, after a location has already been established. In other words, a scene that begins with the shot heading EXT. DODGERS STADIUM - DAY can later include the shot headings NEW ANGLE - SCOREBOARD and ANGLE ON UMPIRE, but not the shot headings NEW ANGLE - PORPOISES AT SEA or ANGLE ON HOLLYWOOD SIGN.

Up angle and down angle

An *up angle* indicates that the camera is shooting upward, while a *down angle* indicates that the camera is shooting down toward its subject:

```
UP ANGLE - GOLIATH

DOWN ANGLE - TINY TIM
```

High angle and low angle

A *high angle* indicates that the camera is placed up high, while a *low angle* indicates that the camera is placed down low:

```
HIGH ANGLE

HIGH ANGLE - LOOKING DOWN ON BATTLEFIELD

LOW ANGLE

LOW ANGLE - LOOKING UP TOWARD ROOFTOPS
```

Reverse angle

A *reverse angle* is used to indicate that we have cut to a shot in which the camera is shooting in the opposite direction from the previous shot. It is used in a sequence like this one:

```
BATTER

swings his bat and connects with the baseball.

REVERSE ANGLE

The ball rockets past the pitcher into centerfield.
```

Here's another example:

```
INT. LIVING ROOM - CHRISTMAS MORNING

The little girl steps through the doorway and looks into
the room with delicious expectation.  But her face
instantly falls.

REVERSE ANGLE - CHRISTMAS TREE

Bare.  All the lights and ornaments are gone.  The
presents too.  Only a scrap of ribbon and a smashed red
bow remain on the floor.
```

POV shot

The *POV shot* is an important one but is often incorrectly formatted in ways that confuse the reader. In a POV shot, the camera is looking through the eyes of a character, which allows the audience to see from that character's *point of view*. It is almost always part of a larger sequence of at least three shots: 1) the shot that shows the character looking at something; 2) the POV shot itself which shows what the character is seeing; and 3) a shot which returns to the main action of the scene. A typical sequence looks like this:

```
EXT. BANKS OF MISSISSIPPI RIVER - MORNING

Huck stares at something moving on the surface of the
water.

HUCK'S POV

A cottonmouth snake swims lazily toward him.

BACK TO SCENE

Huck picks up a rock and grins at the deadly reptile.
```

Also correct:

```
EXT. BANKS OF MISSISSIPPI RIVER - MORNING

Huck stares at something moving on the surface of the
water.

HUCK'S POV - COTTONMOUTH SNAKE

swims lazily toward him.
```

```
HUCK
```
(Here the word HUCK serves as an alternative to BACK TO SCENE.)

```
picks up a rock and grins at the deadly reptile.
```

Another older and rarely used — but entirely correct — formulation for a POV shot is WHAT HE SEES or WHAT HUCK SEES:

```
EXT. BANKS OF MISSISSIPPI RIVER - MORNING

Huck stares at something moving on the surface of the
water.

WHAT HE SEES

A cottonmouth snake swimming lazily toward him.

BACK TO HUCK
```
(BACK TO HUCK is another acceptable alternative to BACK TO SCENE.)

```
He picks up a rock and grins at the deadly reptile.
```

Here is an example of a common mistake:

```
HUCK'S POV - COTTONMOUTH SNAKE

swims lazily toward him.  He picks up a rock and grins
at the deadly reptile.
```

This is incorrect because Huck can't appear in his own POV shot. An important rule: **Once we cut to a POV shot, we're looking directly through the character's eyes and he isn't going to see himself** (except in rare instances when he's seeing his reflection in a mirror, for example, or his image on a store's video monitor). Before we can see Huck, we have to cut to some new shot that includes him, most often Back To Scene or Back To Huck.

Another common and confusing mistake:

```
POV - HUCK
```

Is this Huck's POV, meaning that we're looking through Huck's eyes? Or is this someone else's POV looking at Huck? It's impossible to tell, which is why it's a mistake.

Sometimes a writer wants to call for a POV shot without revealing yet whose POV it is in order to maintain mystery. Here's an example of how to set that up:

        EXT. DARK PARKING LOT - NIGHT

        Rita climbs from her Miata.

        MYSTERY POV

        Watching FROM BEHIND bushes as she walks alone toward
        the lake.

Also correct:

        WATCHER'S POV

        ANONYMOUS POV

        SUBJECTIVE CAMERA

Subjective camera is simply another way of indicating that the camera is looking through a character's eyes.

Specialized types of POV shots include binocular POVs, microscopic POVs, upside-down POVs and POV shots out windows and through sniper scopes. They can be formatted as follows:

        BINOCULAR POV

        SGT. GRIGGS' BINOCULAR POV - ENEMY INFANTRYMEN

        move along the distant ridge.

        MICROSCOPIC POV

        The bacterium slowly divides, then divides again.

        PETER'S UPSIDE-DOWN POV - DANCE FLOOR

        Everyone seems to be dancing on the ceiling.

        PAMELA'S POV - THROUGH WINDOW

        Rain has begun to fall.

        POV SHOT THROUGH SNIPER SCOPE - PRIME MINISTER

        The cross hairs hover over the official.

Handheld shot

A *handheld shot* is one in which the camera is being held by the camera operator to give an added sense of motion, energy or confusion, or to heighten the illusion that we're seeing through a character's eyes in a POV shot:

```
HANDHELD SHOT - MOVING WITH MURPHY

As he runs for his life, breathing hard, sweating like
an iced tea on an August day in Georgia.
```

Also correct:

```
MOVING WITH MURPHY (HANDHELD)
```

Subject of shot

Separate from the type of shot is the *subject of the shot*, meaning the character or object being featured in the shot. The subject is a thing, something concrete and visible. It may be as small as a couple of mice or as enormous as a mountain range:

```
MICKEY AND MINNIE

HIMALAYAS
```

It may include descriptors:

```
CRYING BOY AND HIS SNIFFLING LITTLE SISTER

LAST MAN ON EARTH
```

But no element of a shot heading should include action. The following are incorrect:

```
SLEEPY BOY RUBS HIS EYES

NAVY SEALS CREEP UP BEACH
```

Instead, separate the subject of the shot from the action, like this:

```
SLEEPY BOY

rubs his eyes.

NAVY SEALS

creep up the beach.
```

If a shot has more than one subject, separate the multiple subjects with commas, slashes or the conjunction "and":

```
TRACKING SHOT - MIKE, SAMMY, SAL AND WANDA

THREE SHOT - HANSEL/GRETEL/WITCH

SERGEANT AND TWO CORPORALS

WIDE SHOT - TEX GRIFFIN, HIS PONY AND STONY RIDGE BEYOND
THEM
```

Not:

```
WIDE SHOT - TEX GRIFFIN - HIS PONY - STONY RIDGE BEYOND
THEM
```

Time of Day

A shot heading often indicates what *time of day* a scene is taking place. The most basic designations are Day and Night, and they're important not only for maintaining a reader's orientation within the story but also because they have important practical implications for production.

Day indicates that a scene takes place during daylight.

Night indicates that a scene takes place in the dark.

Magic hour is used to describe the very short period at sunset when the light is waning but the sun has not yet set. It's called magic because it makes for great pictures, but it's also terribly short and so it isn't practical to shoot long scenes under these brief conditions.

Sunset, sunrise and *dusk* are all acceptable designations, but also carry practical limitations for production.

Writers may also indicate a time of day more specifically or colorfully:

```
DEAD OF NIGHT

HIGH NOON

3 AM
```

Other time designations help the reader remain oriented within time, especially when a screenplay's narrative is nonlinear, meaning it doesn't unfold in strictly chronological order:

```
INT. BEDROOM - ON SLEEPING CHILD - 15 MINUTES LATER

EXT. SWIMMING POOL - CONTINUOUS ACTION

EXT. INDEPENDENCE HALL - JULY 4, 1776

EXT. WHITE HOUSE - ESTABLISHING - PRESENT DAY

INT. PENTICUFF HOUSE - GARAGE - FIVE MONTHS EARLIER

INT. SUBWAY CAR - SAME TIME
```

Occasionally, more than one time descriptor is used in a single shot heading. In such cases, **the term that actually describes the time of day comes first, followed in parentheses by the additional modifiers**:

```
EXT. MOGADISHU - WEAPONS MARKET - DAY (AUGUST 5, 1995)

INT. CLASSROOM - NIGHT (CONTINUOUS ACTION)

EXT. BMW DEALERSHIP - SUNRISE (BACK TO PRESENT)
```

The term *Continuous Action* is used to emphasize that one scene follows the preceding one immediately, without any intervening passage of time:

```
INT. HALLWAY

Running for her life, Penelope bangs up against the door
and twists the knob.

INT. DOCTOR'S OFFICE WAITING ROOM - CONTINUOUS ACTION

Her eyes wild, Penelope stumbles inside, desperate to
find a friendly face.
```

CONTINUOUS ACTION can sometimes be useful to make clear to the reader that no time has passed between shots or scenes, but it is often overused. In the example above, context makes fairly obvious that the action from one shot to the next is continuous. The use of CONTINUOUS ACTION adds little. It simply clutters the page with unnecessary words. A cleaner, crisper style results when CONTINUOUS ACTION is used rarely, and only when added clarity is required.

Various additional descriptors are also lumped into the "time of day" category, even though they have nothing to do with the actual time of day. They include terms describing weather (*rain, snow, sleet*, etc.), the quality of the film or video stock being used (*black and white, 8 mm, home video, newsreel footage*, etc.), *slow motion*, and *MOS*, an old Hollywood term with an amusing history. MOS indicates a scene filmed without sound. Hollywood folklore holds that this term arose from German directors working in early Hollywood who in their limited English would order a scene shot "mit-out sound," duly noted on the script as "MOS."

```
EXT. DISNEYLAND - NEAR SPLASH MOUNTAIN - DAY (HOME
VIDEO)

EXT. DALLAS BOOK DESPOSITORY - ON JFK IN OPEN
CONVERTIBLE - DAY (BLACK AND WHITE)

INT. THEATER - ON STAGE - NIGHT (MOS)

The actors go through their motions.  Mouths move
appropriately.  Singers sing.  Dancers dance.  But we
hear nothing of it.  Only the disembodied PLINK, PLINK,
PLINK of a TOY PIANO coming from who knows where.

EXT. CENTRAL PARK - CHRISTMAS NIGHT (SNOW)

INT. ORIENT EXPRESS - DAY (RAIN)

EXT. CHICAGO WORLD'S FAIR - DAY (NEWSREEL FOOTAGE)

CLOSE ON BULLET (SLOW MOTION)

EXT. RACE TRACK - AIRBORNE STOCK CAR - DAY (SLOW MOTION)

CHILD'S BIRTHDAY PARTY - DAY (1966) (8MM)
```

Note in the examples above that the term describing the actual time of day comes first, followed by the additional modifier or modifiers in parentheses.

How to arrange the information in a shot heading

As we've seen, a shot heading can contain information in up to five distinct categories: 1) interior or exterior; 2) location; 3) type of shot; 4) subject of shot; and 5) time of day. **The information should be presented in exactly that order.**

```
[1]INT. [2]FUNHOUSE - [3]MED. SHOT - [4]MR. WHIPPLE - [5]NIGHT
```

Very long shot headings are possible that contain a relatively large amount of information in each of the five of categories:

```
[1]INT. [2]FUNHOUSE - COLLAPSING REAR SECTION - HALL OF
MIRRORS - [3]SLOW TRACKING SHOT - [4]MR. WHIPPLE, MRS.
WHIPPLE AND YOUNG WINSTEAD WHIPPLE - [5]NIGHT (CONTINUOUS
ACTION) (BLACK AND WHITE)
```

44

But notice that even in this unnaturally long and ungainly shot heading, the information is laid out according to the same simple plan.

Of course many shot headings contain information from only one or a few of the five possible categories. Here, the rule is the same. Simply lay out what you have in the established order:

[1]INT. [2]FUNHOUSE - [5]NIGHT

[3]MED. SHOT - [4]MR. WHIPPLE

[4]WHIPPLE

How to decide what information to include in shot headings

Writers sometimes wonder how much information should be included in shot headings. Many writers include too much information, much of it redundant, making the screenplay cluttered and difficult to read. Other writers fail to provide enough information, which can leave the reader confused. **The goal when composing a shot heading should be to provide the necessary information clearly and concisely, including just enough words to do the job but no more.** Here are three general guidelines to help you decide how much information is enough, and which will go a great distance toward reducing the length of your shot headings:

1. **At the beginning of a sequence that takes place in a new location or after a passage of time, indicate INT. or EXT. and a description of the location, along with an indication of the time of day:**

   INT. WHITE HOUSE - OVAL OFFICE - DAY

   These are often called *master shot headings*.

2. **If specific shots follow a master shot heading and occur in the same location and within the same time frame, it isn't necessary to repeat the location and time of day.**

   The master shot heading above could be followed by shots like these:

   ANGLE ON PRESIDENT'S DESK

   MED. SHOT - PRESIDENT BARTLETT

   LEO

3. **Shot headings should be as short as possible.**

   In general, the readability of a script increases as the word count decreases. That's why rule #2 above is important. Endlessly repeating something like INT. WHITE HOUSE -

OVAL OFFICE as part of each of the minor shot headings turns a simple thing like LEO into the jawbreaker INT. WHITE HOUSE - OVAL OFFICE - LEO - DAY. Not only is this shot heading far more work to read, it obscures the most important element in the shot — Leo. It also breaks up the continuity of the ongoing master scene and suggests that a time cut may have occurred. All of this slows, confuses and potentially irritates the busy reader.

Information about the type of shot can also frequently be omitted. Rarely is it necessary to indicate FULL SHOT - LEO or MED. SHOT - LEO, rather than simply LEO. When it is necessary to the telling of the story to call a specific type of shot, such as a POV shot or a close shot, by all means do it. But **when there is no strongly compelling reason to specify a particular type of shot, don't.** Leave it to the director.

How to decide when to create a new shot heading

Including too many shot headings or too few often creates problems for writers and readers alike. Too many shot headings clutter a screenplay and can make a writer appear amateurish. Too few shot headings leave the reader confused and create headaches when production approaches. **In general, insert a new shot heading only when necessary.** Three rules of thumb provide guidance here:

1. **Insert a shot heading when there is a change in location or time.**

    Let's say we're inside the Oval Office (INT. OVAL OFFICE - DAY), and then cut outside to the Lincoln Memorial. We would need a new shot heading along these lines: EXT. LINCOLN MEMORIAL - DAY. That's fairly straightforward.

    Now let's say we're in the Oval Office, then we cut to another scene in the same location, but it's 90 minutes later. We need a new shot heading, something like this: INT. OVAL OFFICE - 90 MINUTES LATER or SAME - 90 MINUTES LATER.

    Writers sometimes get into trouble when a character moves from one location to another. The following is incorrect:

    ```
    INT. JOSIAH'S MOTOR HOME - NIGHT

    The old guy pours himself a cup of coffee and steps
    outside.  He climbs painfully to the ground and looks up
    at the stars.
    ```

    We're missing a shot heading that accounts for Josiah's movement from an interior location to an exterior one, which may be shot at a completely different time and place. The sequence should be set up like this:

```
INT. JOSIAH'S MOTOR HOME - NIGHT

The old guy pours himself a cup of coffee and steps
outside.

EXT. MOTOR HOME - NIGHT

He climbs painfully to the ground and looks up at the
stars.
```

2. **Add shot headings when necessary for the visual telling of the story.**

Among the screenwriter's tasks is creating the visual experience of the screen story in the imagination of the reader. Shot headings are one of the essential tools for accomplishing this task. We have already discussed what many of these shots are: POV shots, close shots, wide shots, tracking shots, up angles, down angles and so forth. If visual attention must be focused very specifically on a small object or detail, an extreme close shot serves precisely that purpose and is appropriate and justified. At other times, say in an ordinary dialogue scene between two characters, it might not be necessary to call attention to any particular visual detail and only the initial master shot heading is required. Add shot headings of the more visually specific sort only when you have a compelling visual reason for doing so.

3. **Add shot headings when logic requires it.**

Sometimes plain logic requires a new shot heading. For example, after the shot heading WILMA'S POV, a new shot heading, such as BACK TO SCENE, is logically required before Wilma can appear again on screen. Similarly, after an EXTREME CLOSEUP ON GNAT'S LITTLE TOE, logic requires a new shot heading before the expanse of the Grand Canyon may appear on screen.

4. **Don't add a shot heading where there is no new shot.**

Sometimes writers set up as a shot heading what is really just a movement of the camera. The following is incorrect:

```
INT. SUBMARINE - GALLEY - NIGHT

Nason and his guys fight the fire.  They know that at
this depth, they're fighting for their lives.  But
they're choking on the smoke.  And they're losing the
battle.

PAN TO ENSIGN MENENDEZ

Leading in a fresh contingent of men to join the fight.
```

47

The pan is really just a camera move within the existing shot and shouldn't logically be given a new shot heading. Instead, format the sequence like this:

```
INT. SUBMARINE - GALLEY - NIGHT

Nason and his guys fight the fire.  They know that at
this depth, they're fighting for their lives.  But
they're choking on the smoke.  And they're losing the
battle.  PAN TO Ensign Menendez, leading in a fresh
contingent of men to join the fight.
```

Other common camera moves that don't logically warrant new shot headings include RACK FOCUS TO, TILT or PAN TO REVEAL and ZOOM or TRACK TO.

An important exception to this rule occurs when we start on a closeup or an extreme closeup and pull back to reveal that we're in a whole new location. For practical reasons (namely, that production personnel need a new master shot heading to go with the new location), a new shot heading is added.

Instead of this:

```
EXTREME CLOSEUP - WOMAN'S FIST

opens to show she holds a house key.  She inserts it in
a doorknob.  PULL BACK to reveal Dotty opening the front
door of Frank's house.  Dotty lets herself in.
```

Do this:

```
EXTREME CLOSEUP - WOMAN'S FIST

opens to show she holds a house key.  She inserts it in
a doorknob.  PULL BACK to reveal:

EXT. FRANK'S HOUSE

Dotty opens the front door and lets herself in.
```

5.   **Add shot headings to break up long passages of action and lend a sense of increased tempo.**

The problem: Because of the narrow column that even intermittent dialogue makes down the center of the script page, a screenplay often contains a great deal of white space. Add in the space around shot headings, scene transitions and a few short paragraphs, and a typical script page contains relatively few words, looks spacious and reads fairly breezily. By contrast, action sequences, arguably the fastest-paced sequences written for the

48

screen, can appear in a script like dull blocks of words crowding the page. Ironically, then, when an action sequence obliterates too much of the white space, action can end up reading so slowly that readers are tempted to skim it or even skip it entirely.

The solution: Break up the action with short shot headings to restore white space and help guide the reader's eye down the page. Compare the following sequences, the first with only a single master shot heading and the second with additional shot headings inserted to break up the page.

```
INT. PARKING STRUCTURE - DAY

The immaculate MOTOR HOME ROARS down the ramp into the
underground garage, followed by three squad cars.
Michael cranks the steering wheel hard to the right and
the MOTOR HOME makes a SQUEALING turn.  Ahead, a
concrete beam hangs low.  Too low for the high-profile
vehicle.  Michael ducks at the moment of IMPACT.  The
ROOF PEELS OFF the motor home with a METALLIC SHRIEK.
The crumpled SHEET METAL BANGS off the hood of a
pursuing squad car.  One of the cops slings a RIOT GUN
out his window and FIRES.  The GLASS in Michael's WINDOW
EXPLODES.  He makes a desperation left turn down another
ramp but cuts the corner too close.  A long slab of
METAL CURLS AWAY from the side of the motor home like an
orange peel.  Michael plunges his giant convertible
deeper into the garage, his hair blowing in the open
air.  At the bottom of the ramp, steel pipes crisscross
the low ceiling.  What's left of the MOTOR HOME GRINDS
against them and debris flies as the big vehicle gets
chopped down even shorter.  Shreds of insulation,
stuffed animals and cooking utensils fill the air.  A
microwave oven bounces onto the hood of a squad car and
SMASHES THROUGH the WINDSHIELD, landing in the empty
passenger seat.  Michael finds a ramp sloping up toward
daylight and heads for freedom, no longer pursued,
piloting the decimated chassis of what was once his
proud home.
```

While this might be fun to watch on screen, it looks fairly awful on the page. Here is the same action broken up with intermediate shot headings that correspond roughly to the various smaller pieces of action that make up the whole sequence:

```
INT. PARKING STRUCTURE - DAY

The immaculate MOTOR HOME ROARS down the ramp into the
underground garage, followed by three squad cars.
```

MICHAEL

cranks the steering wheel hard to the right and:

MOTOR HOME

makes a SQUEALING turn. Ahead, a concrete beam hangs
low. Too low for the high-profile vehicle.

MICHAEL

ducks at the moment of IMPACT. The ROOF PEELS OFF the
motor home with a METALLIC SHRIEK.

CRUMPLED SHEET METAL

BANGS off the hood of a pursuing squad car. One of the
cops slings a RIOT GUN out his window and FIRES.

ON MICHAEL

As the GLASS in his WINDOW EXPLODES. He makes a
desperation left turn down another ramp but cuts the
corner too close.

LONG SLAB OF METAL

CURLS AWAY from the side of the motor home like an
orange peel.

MICHAEL

plunges his giant convertible deeper into the garage,
his hair blowing in the open air.

AT BOTTOM OF RAMP

Steel pipes crisscross the low ceiling. What's left of
the MOTOR HOME GRINDS against them and debris flies as
the big vehicle gets chopped down even shorter.

BEHIND MOTOR HOME

Shreds of insulation, stuffed animals and cooking
utensils fill the air. A microwave oven bounces onto
the hood of a squad car and SMASHES through the
WINDSHIELD, landing in the empty passenger seat.

```
MICHAEL

finds a ramp sloping up toward daylight and heads for
freedom, no longer pursued, piloting the decimated
chassis of what was once his proud home.
```

The passage now looks like an action sequence and reads like one. This layout also gives production personnel the material they're going to be shooting in more manageable bites. The downside for the writer battling to keep a script's page count down is that this style uses about twice as much space as leaving the text in a single block.

An important caution: For all of the reasons noted above, not every page in a screenplay should be sprinkled with so many shot headings. Use this shot heading style sparingly and only when it's genuinely justified.

What NOT to include in a shot heading

Shot headings should not include any of the following:

1. **Sounds or sound effects.**

   Sounds and sound effects belong in direction, not shot headings.

2. **Action.**

   A shot heading is like a noun. It is the subject or headline of the shot. The action belongs beneath the shot heading in direction, like this:

   ```
   MICHAEL

   grips the steering wheel.
   ```

   Not:

   ```
   MICHAEL GRIPS STEERING WHEEL
   ```

3. **The articles *The, A* or *An.***

   Shot headings avoid using articles in order to save space. Instead of writing CLOSE ON THE MAN'S HAND, it is standard to write CLOSE ON MAN'S HAND. Instead of EXT. THE BAKERY, write simply EXT. BAKERY.

   Occasionally, omitting an article causes a shot heading to read awkwardly. In those cases, it is acceptable to include the article.

Formatting specialized sequences

Certain specialized sequences, such as flashbacks, dream sequences, split screens and telephone intercuts, require special treatment.

Flashbacks and dream sequences

A *flashback* is a scene or series of scenes that takes place prior to the story's main action. A *dream sequence* is, naturally, a scene or series of scenes that takes place in a dream. **In a flashback, the word "flashback" appears underlined as the very first element in the shot heading, followed by a hyphen**:

FLASHBACK - INT. FUNHOUSE - NIGHT

A dream sequence is set up the same way:

DREAM SEQUENCE - INT. FUNHOUSE - NIGHT

Writer John August (*Big Fish, Charlie and the Chocolate Factory*) suggests a different approach which he uses, and which passes the tests of clarity and economy:

INT. FUNHOUSE - NIGHT [FLASHBACK]

Alternative, more recent terms sometimes used to introduce short flashbacks are *memory hit* and *memory flash*:

MEMORY HIT - CORVETTE

careens out of control.

MEMORY FLASH

Melissa's face the instant before impact.

Imagination sequences can be handled like dream sequences:

IAN'S IMAGINATION - INT. CIRCUS TENT

Ending a flashback or dream sequence

When a flashback or dream sequence ends, you have three choices. You can simply move on to the next scene:

DREAM SEQUENCE - EXT. FERRIS WHEEL - DAY

Josh dangles by his fingertips from the highest car.
Melanie sits in the car above him, prying his fingers
loose one by one. And suddenly, Josh is falling,
falling, falling...

INT. SCIENCE CLASSROOM - DAY

Josh jerks his head up off his desk, jolting awake. He
looks across the room at Melanie with deep suspicion.

Here, the context makes obvious that the dream has ended and no further formatting cues are required. Other less obvious situations benefit from a more explicit indication that the flashback or dream is over. This is the second method of ending a flashback or dream sequence:

DREAM SEQUENCE - EXT. FERRIS WHEEL - DAY

Josh dangles by his fingertips from the highest car.
Melanie sits in the car above him, prying his fingers
loose one by one. And suddenly, Josh is falling,
falling, falling...

                              END DREAM SEQUENCE.

INT. SCIENCE CLASSROOM - DAY

Melanie looks up from her book and notices that Josh is
looking at her sort of cock-eyed, like he's just woken
up. He appears deeply, darkly suspicious.

A flashback can also be handled this same way:

FLASHBACK - EXT. RIVERBANK

Charity stands watching the big riverboat burn, her
hands over her mouth. Slowly she collapses in the mud.

EXT. SMALL-TOWN CEMETERY

A half-dozen funerals underway simultaneously. The
scope of the tragedy hits home. Charity stands at a
fresh grave, grieving her sister alone.

                              END FLASHBACK.

INT. CHARITY'S BEDROOM - NIGHT

```
She stares at her image in the mirror.
```

A third way to indicate that a flashback has ended is to add the words BACK TO PRESENT to the shot heading that immediately follows the flashback:

```
FLASHBACK - EXT. RIVERBANK

Charity stands watching the big riverboat burn, her
hands over her mouth.  Slowly she collapses in the mud.

EXT. SMALL-TOWN CEMETERY

A half-dozen funerals underway simultaneously.  The
scope of the tragedy hits home.  Charity stands at a
fresh grave, grieving her sister alone.

INT. CHARITY'S BEDROOM - NIGHT (BACK TO PRESENT)

She stares at her image in the mirror.
```

Note that FLASHBACK is one word and that it appears only once, as does DREAM SEQUENCE, at the beginning of the sequence, even if the sequence consists of multiple scenes.

Montages and series of shots

A *montage* is a series of brief images, often under music, used to show the passage of time, the unfolding of a character's plan or the evolution of a character or relationship over time. A *series of shots* performs a similar function. Though purists will argue that there is an important difference between the two, that argument is beyond the scope of this guide. From a formatting standpoint, they are twins.

A montage includes the word MONTAGE in the shot heading. A series of shots includes the words SERIES OF SHOTS in the heading.

In either case, the shot heading is followed by a description of the content of the various shots that make up the montage or series of shots. Here is a montage:

```
AROUND PARIS - MONTAGE

Jim and Angela sit at a café, sipping coffee, tentative
with one another.

They walk through the Musee D'Orsay, pausing in front of
a Van Gogh, lost in animated conversation.  They seem
surprised at what they're discovering in each other.
```

They climb the endless iron stairs of the Eiffel Tower.
She's getting tired. He offers his hand. She takes it
and he pulls her along.

They stand on the Pont Neuf, gazing together at the
waters of the Seine flowing beneath them. The sun is
setting. Angela looks into Jim's eyes. She goes up on
her toes and gives him a tender first kiss.

Here is a series of shots:

SERIES OF SHOTS

John ransacks the glove compartment of the old Dodge.
He comes out with a book of matches.

He searches and finds a newspaper in a pile of trash
behind the house.

He rips the paper and crumples it into tight balls.

He stuffs the paper in the dark space beneath the house.

He strikes a match and sets fire to the crumpled paper.

He sits in the Dodge, watching the house burn.

Each paragraph represents a shot within the montage or series of shots. This is the simplest
formatting method. An alternative is to assign each shot within the montage or series of shots its
own shot heading. The shots are then lettered alphabetically and the individual shot headings and
descriptions are indented three spaces from the normal left margin:

AROUND PARIS - MONTAGE

A) EXT. CAFÉ - DAY

   Jim and Angela sit sipping coffee, tentative with one
   another.

B) INT. MUSEE D'ORSAY - DAY

   They walk through the museum, pausing in front of a
   Van Gogh, lost in animated conversation. They seem
   surprised at what they're discovering in each other.

C) EXT. EIFFEL TOWER - DAY

    They climb the endless iron stairs of the Eiffel
    Tower. She's getting tired. He offers his hand. She
    takes it and he pulls her along.

D) EXT. SEINE RIVER - DUSK

    They stand on the Pont Neuf, gazing together at the
    waters of the Seine flowing beneath them. The sun is
    setting. Angela looks into Jim's eyes. She goes up
    on her toes and gives him a tender first kiss.

Both of these methods make clear what is the content of each individual shot, and which shots are included in the montage or series of shots, and there is no confusion about where the montage or series of shots ends.

Intercut sequences

An *intercut sequence* is one that cuts alternately between two or more locations, most often to present all parties to a telephone conversation. Each location must be established with its own shot heading, and the instruction INTERCUT must be given. Thereafter, dialogue can flow as if all the characters are present together and (V.O.) is not indicated beside any of the character names over dialogue:

INT. MARYANN'S KITCHEN - MORNING

She dials the phone.

INT. MARK'S OFFICE - SAME TIME

His PHONE begins to RING. He crosses to pick it up.

                MARK
        Mark Markisian and Associates.

INTERCUT telephone conversation.

                MARYANN
      Mark? It's Maryann. How are
      you?

                MARK
      Fantastic. I'm so glad you
      called. The messenger just
      brought your cashier's check.

Here is another way to format the same conversation:

```
INT. MARYANN'S KITCHEN - MORNING

She dials the phone. INTERCUT WITH:

INT. MARK'S OFFICE - SAME TIME

His PHONE begins to RING.  He crosses to pick it up.

                    MARK
          Mark Markisian and Associates.

                    MARYANN
          Mark?  It's Maryann.  How are
          you?

                    MARK
          Fantastic.  I'm so glad you
          called.  The messenger just
          brought your cashier's check.
```

Text messages and instant messages, caller ID and email

These can be played in direction, don't require special shot headings, and are described in the chapter on "Direction."

Split screen sequences

A *split screen sequence* consists of two or more scenes simultaneously sharing the screen, which may be split into left and right halves, or four quadrants, or an entire checkerboard of smaller images. A two-location split screen gets a shot heading like this:

```
INT. GAS STATION BATHROOM/INT. FIFTH AVENUE LAW OFFICE -
SPLIT SCREEN - DAY

Milo, dressed in nothing but his boxers, has his cell
phone out and is waving it around the filthy john,
trying desperately to get a signal.  Back at the office,
his entire staff is searching just as desperately for
the missing report.
```

Capitalizing McDonald's and DeVries in shot headings

When names like McDonald's and DeVries appear in a shot heading, capitalize like this for greater readability:

```
INT. McDONALD'S RESTAURANT - CLOSE ON DeVRIES
     (The c in McDonald's and the e in DeVries are lower-cased.)
```

Breaking a page after a shot heading

Never break a page immediately after a shot heading. Always include at least one complete sentence of direction or one line of dialogue before breaking the page:

```
EXT. MOTOCROSS COURSE - DAY

The BIKES ROAR past.
-----page break -----
A cloud of dust fills the air in their wake.
```

An exception to this rule occurs when a shot heading stands alone as a scene:

```
EXT. McGREGOR MANSION - NIGHT (ESTABLISHING SHOT)
-----page break-----
INT. McGREGOR MANSION - NIGHT

The party is in progress.
```

Spacing between shots and scenes

Standard practice allows for either double spacing (one blank line) or triple spacing (two blank lines) before each new shot heading. You can do it like this:

```
EXT. COFFEE SHOP - DAY

Mick and Minn walk in.

INT. COFFEE SHOP - DAY

They sit down.
```

Or like this:

```
EXT. COFFEE SHOP - DAY

Mick and Minn walk in.


INT. COFFEE SHOP - DAY

They sit down.
```

The first method allows more material to fit on the page. The second method leaves more white space and looks more inviting to the reader.

A third method triple spaces before master scene headings and double spaces before each new shot heading within a master scene:

```
INT. COFFEE SHOP - DAY

They sit down.  Mick notices something on the table.

INSERT - TABLETOP

Something scratched into the finish.  The letters X, G
and Z.

BACK TO SCENE

He frowns.  Jots the letters on a napkin.


EXT. COFFEE SHOP

Mick runs for his car.


INT. POLICE PRECINCT

Mick strides in.
```

A rogues' gallery of nonstandard shot headings

All of the following shot headings are out of standard format. After each heading, an explanation of the problem is given, along with a corrected version of the shot heading:

EXT. MERCEDES - INTERSTATE 70
  (Follow the general-to-specific rule: EXT. INTERSTATE 70 - MERCEDES.)

EXT. APARTMENT - SPRING - 1965 - DAWN
  (You only get one main time-of-day designation, with the others following in parentheses: EXT. APARTMENT - DAWN (SPRING 1965).)

INT. TENEMENT APARTMENT - DETROIT - NIGHT
  (The city name should be placed inside parentheses: INT. TENEMENT APARTMENT (DETROIT) - NIGHT.)

INT. PLAYBOY MANSION/KITCHEN - DAY
  (As you move from general to specific, separate the location elements with a hyphen: INT. PLAYBOY MANSION - KITCHEN - DAY.)

EXT. THE FRONT OF THE BAR
  (Omit the articles: EXT. FRONT OF BAR.)

ANGLE ON BLENDER SPINNING AND SPINNING
  (Remove the action from the shot heading: ANGLE ON BLENDER, with "Spinning and spinning" placed beneath the shot heading in direction.)

MONTAGE
  (Only flashbacks and dream sequences get underlined: MONTAGE.)

CLOSE ON: ASTRONAUT JOHN GLENN
  (Lose the colon: CLOSE ON ASTRONAUT JOHN GLENN.)

Angle on:

Mike lifting the heavy beam off Otto.
  (Ouch. Do it like this: ANGLE ON MIKE, with "Lifting the heavy beam off Otto" placed beneath the shot heading in direction.)

EXT. LAUNCH PAD -- SPACE SHUTTLE ENDEAVOR -- CONTINUOUS
  (Separate the elements with a single hyphen (space hyphen space), not a dash: EXT. LAUNCH PAD - SPACE SHUTTLE ENDEAVOR - CONTINUOUS.)

I./E. MOLLY'S VW - DAY
  (Spell it out: INT./EXT. MOLLY'S VW - DAY.)

INT. - PHONE BOOTH - MOMENTS LATER
  (There's no hyphen after Int. or Ext.: INT. PHONE BOOTH - MOMENTS LATER.)

EXT. PHIL'S APARTMENT - HALLWAY
>   (The hallway is really an interior location which happens to be outside Phil's apartment: INT. HALLWAY - OUTSIDE PHIL'S APARTMENT.)

A LONG STRETCH OF DESERT HIGHWAY - ARIZONA DESERT - NOON
>   (Lose the article "A" and put the location in order from general to specific: EXT. ARIZONA DESERT - LONG STRETCH OF DESERT HIGHWAY - NOON.)

INT. - MED. SHOT - BECKMAN - DAY
>   (An INT. or EXT. designation requires a location: INT. RESTAURANT - MED. SHOT - BECKMAN - DAY.)

A LOUD BANG
>   (Sounds don't belong in shot headings. You can't photograph a loud bang. What do we see?)

EXT. DOWNTOWN CHICAGO - A HOT JULY AFTERNOON - MUSIC OVER
>   (Lose the article "A" and drop the "MUSIC OVER" down into direction beneath the shot heading: EXT. DOWNTOWN CHICAGO - HOT JULY AFTERNOON.)

CLOSE - ON YOUNG ENGLISH BOY
>   (Don't put a hyphen between CLOSE and ON: CLOSE ON YOUNG ENGLISH BOY.)

INT. BASEMENT, VICTOR'S PLACE
>   (The location always reads from general to specific and its parts are separated by hyphens: INT. VICTOR'S PLACE - BASEMENT.)

MED. SHOT
>   (Of what? MED. SHOT - BRONCO BILLY.)

INT. EXTREME WIDE ANGLE - LIVING ROOM - DAY
>   (Follow the established order of shot heading elements: INT. LIVING ROOM - EXTREME WIDE ANGLE - DAY.)

REVERSE ANGLE - EXT. COW PASTURE
>   (Again, follow the established order: EXT. COW PASTURE - REVERSE ANGLE.)

FAQs about shot headings

Does it worry you or your wife, I mean on a personal level, that you've written nearly 40 pages about shot headings?

It worries me a great deal. But my wife was worried long before.

What is master scene format? Is that the correct format for a spec script?

Master scene format refers to a screenwriting style that employs a minimum of shot headings, just one per scene, which indicate only the location of the scene and the time of day, something like INT. FLINTSTONE HOUSE - NIGHT or EXT. ROSE PARADE - DAY. Strictly speaking, a script written entirely in master scene format would never include slug lines for individual shots. Those individual shots or images might be implied by the way direction is written, but they'd never be called out in shot headings. Some say that a spec script should be written this way. It's not terrible advice, but it isn't quite right. Yes, a script, whether written on spec or progressing through production, should be formatted with as few shot headings as possible. And yes, too many individual shots can bog down a script. But there are times that shot headings other than masters should be used. And screenwriters need not write with a hand tied unnecessarily behind their backs.

I'm a writer-director, and I know exactly how I'm going to shoot each scene. Can't I write in all my shots so readers can visualize my movie the way I see it? I want to prove that I'm the perfect person to direct my film.

If you add all those shot headings, you'll make your script unreadable. All you'll prove is that you don't know how to write a professional screenplay.

You've listed pages and pages of different kinds of shots. I feel totally intimidated. I'm not a cinematographer. Am I supposed to be using all these different kinds of shots (medium shot, two shot, tracking shot)?

No. I'm sure I've never used a medium shot in my life. You want as spare a screenwriting style as you can manage, which might mean writing an entire screenplay without a CUT TO: or POV shot. But there are times a writer working in the increasingly visual media of film and television needs to communicate a particular shot with great specificity because that shot, one the writer sees as clearly as he sees his most intimately drawn character, serves to tell his story as surely as do dialogue and direction. For that reason, this guide includes instructions on how to use those shots in a clear, professional manner. But don't misunderstand. They don't all have to be used in every script. On the contrary. Use them only when they're essential to the telling of your story.

DIRECTION

Also called *action* and *description*, direction consists of passages that describe what is being seen and heard within the shot or scene. It may include *introductions* and *descriptions of characters*, description of characters' actions and demeanor, *sounds* and *sound effects*, *visual effects* and *camera direction*. In short, direction tells us what's happening.

Direction is always written in the present tense:

> Lydia leaps from the precipice and free-falls down the
> cliff face, counting seven agonizing seconds before
> pulling the rip chord. A second later, the yellow
> canopy blossoms above her.

Not:

> Lydia leapt from the precipice and free-fell down the
> cliff face, counting seven agonizing seconds before
> pulling the rip chord. A second later, the yellow
> canopy blossomed above her.

Direction also tends to be written in relatively short, direct sentences designed to paint pictures using the fewest possible words.

Paragraphing in direction

All of the direction beneath a shot heading may be kept together in a single paragraph:

> Lydia hits the ground and rolls. She's immediately
> jerked back to her feet as the canopy is caught in the
> wind. She fights to free herself from the canopy. She
> pulls a knife and slashes at its cords. Something moves
> in the brush behind her. Lydia cuts herself free and
> the canopy blows away in the wind. She turns toward the
> brush, the knife in front of her.

Or it may be broken into several smaller paragraphs:

> Lydia hits the ground and rolls. She's immediately
> jerked back to her feet as the canopy is caught in the
> wind.

```
Lydia fights to free herself from the canopy.  She pulls
a knife and slashes at its cords.

Something moves in the brush behind her.

Lydia cuts herself free and the canopy blows away in the
wind.  She turns toward the brush, the knife in front of
her.
```

The advantages of breaking large passages of direction into smaller paragraphs are that it makes the text more readable, increases the reader's sense of pace and creates white space that helps the page look less dense and imposing. A further important advantage is that skillful and judicious use of paragraphing in direction allows the writer to direct the reader's visual imagination without resorting to a large number of shot headings. Notice how a sequence of specific visuals can be implied without adding individual shot headings:

```
Billy unlatches the tackle box and looks inside.

His finger sweep aside a tangle of lures and knotted
fishing line to uncover the missing penny.

A look of wonder spreads over Billy's face.
```

The disadvantage to this style is that it takes more space, increasing the page count of the script (though not as much as does breaking the scene with additional shot headings). An effective screenwriting style balances these often competing considerations.

Paragraphs of direction are never indented:

```
Lydia hits the ground and rolls.  She's immediately
jerked back to her feet as the canopy is caught in the
wind.
```

Breaking a page in the middle of direction

Never break a page in the middle of a sentence in direction. When breaking direction, always split the page between sentences:

```
EXT. MOTOCROSS COURSE - DAY

The BIKES ROAR past.
-----page break -----
A cloud of dust fills the air in their wake.
```

Not:

```
EXT. MOTOCROSS COURSE - DAY

The BIKES ROAR past.  A cloud of dust fills the air in
-----page break -----
their wake.
```

Capitalization in direction

Standard script format dictates that words in direction are typed in all capital letters if they're performing one of only three tasks: 1) *introducing a speaking character*; 2) *describing sound effects and offscreen sounds*; or 3) *describing camera direction*.

```
¹MACK HUMPHREYS runs through the door.  ²FLAMES ROAR all
around him.  ³CAMERA PUSHES IN CLOSE ON his terrified
face.
```

Introducing a speaking character

The first time a speaking character appears on screen, the character's name is typed in all capitals:

```
Dressed in his full space suit, JOHN GLENN steps out of
the launch tower elevator.  Launch workers surround
Glenn and help him toward the waiting spacecraft.
```

Note in the example above that the second time Glenn's name appears, it is not typed in all capitals. **Each speaking character's name should be typed in all capitals once and only once.**

Even if a speaking character's name isn't a proper name, it still gets capitalized when the character first appears. Subsequently the first letter of the character name gets capitalized every time it appears:

```
A stunning BALLERINA steps before the stage lights.  The
Ballerina curtseys and begins to dance.
```

Many times, a character will be described somewhat generically, as a "woman" or a "firefighter," before her name appears in direction. As long as the proper name appears fairly quickly after the generic reference, wait and capitalize just the proper name:

```
A firefighter runs through the door.  Her name is LORI
HEDDEN.  The fire burns hot all around her.  She's
terrified.
```

However, if the firefighter speaks before we know her name, we have no choice but to capitalize the word "firefighter" and then, later, her proper name once we learn it:

```
A FIREFIGHTER runs through the door.

                    FIREFIGHTER
          Anybody in here?

The fire burns hot all around her.  She's terrified.
Her name is LORI HEDDEN.

                    LORI (FIREFIGHTER)
          Anybody?!
```

Don't be fooled by a character name that shows up before the character does. Wait to capitalize the name until the character himself appears onscreen:

```
Launch workers gather around the tower elevator, waiting
for John Glenn to emerge.  The door slides to the side
and GLENN steps out in his full space suit.
```

If a speaking character first appears in a shot heading, capitalize the next reference within direction:

```
REVERSE ANGLE - JOHN GLENN

steps off the elevator in his full space suit.  Launch
workers gather around GLENN.
```

If a character doesn't have any lines, don't capitalize his name. (A rare exception is made for a major character who doesn't speak but nevertheless has a significant, ongoing role in the story.) Typing a character's name in all capitals tells production personnel that the character has lines, which has significant ramifications for casting and budget. Any number of nonspeaking characters can be introduced in a paragraph of direction without anything getting capitalized, until we finally get to a speaking character:

```
Inside the big top, clowns direct the audience to their
seats.  A midget walks on tiny stilts.  A lion tamer
works his big cats in a giant cage.  Seven Russian
acrobats fly through the air.  A popcorn vendor hawks
his wares.  Girls covered in gaudy sequins ride
elephants.  And in the center ring, the MASTER OF
CEREMONIES calls into his microphone:

                    MASTER OF CEREMONIES
          Ladies and gentlemen, boys and
          girls --
```

How to handle the reintroduction of a speaking character who appears at various ages

Sometimes we meet a character at a given age, say 20 years old, and then meet the same character as a 70-year-old. Does the character's name get capitalized a second time when the 70-year-old version is introduced? The answer depends on whether or not one actor is expected to play both roles. Capitalizing the second introduction implies that a different actor will play the second role. In the movie *A Beautiful Mind*, actor Russell Crowe plays John Nash at many different ages throughout the character's life, from a young student arriving at college to an old man receiving a Nobel Prize. Because the same actor plays the character of John Nash at all of those different ages, Nash would properly be introduced and his name typed in all capitals just one time, when the character of the young student first appears on screen. In the movie *Big Fish*, the main character is played by two actors. Ewan McGregor plays the young man while Albert Finney plays the older man. This character's name would be introduced and capitalized twice, once for each actor. Often it's an easy call. We meet a character at ages 7 and 37. No question. Two different actors. Or we encounter a character at ages 25 and 40. Almost certainly the same actor.

For an example of how a character gets re-introduced when played at a second age by a second actor, let's pretend that *A Beautiful Mind* contains a flashback to John Nash's childhood. We'll see his name capitalized when he's introduced as a college student, and then when he's introduced as a child:

```
An awkward young man makes his way among the brilliant
and urbane young mathematicians: JOHN NASH.  He's
smarter than all of them and he's the only one who knows
it.  As he takes in the faces of the competition --

FLASHBACK - EXT. WEST VIRGINIA SCHOOLHOUSE - DAY (1935)

An awkward little boy steps onto the yard of a
ramshackle mountain schoolhouse.  It's YOUNG NASH, age
8.  The raw-boned sons of coal miners stare at this odd
boy.
```

YOUNG NASH could just as correctly be called 8-YEAR-OLD NASH, YOUNG JOHN NASH, JOHNNY NASH, or any other name that wouldn't reasonably get confused with Nash in his adult incarnation.

Describing sound effects and offscreen sounds

The second reason for typing words in all capital letters in direction is because they describe a sound effect or an offscreen sound. Three basic rules govern capitalization for sound effects and offscreen sounds:

1.   **Type *all sounds* that originate <u>offscreen</u> in all capital letters.** This includes everything

from a ticking clock to a woman's scream to a nuclear explosion, no exceptions.

```
From somewhere O.S. comes the sound of a WOMAN'S SCREAM.

FOOTSTEPS can be heard in the room overhead.

The MOAN of a CAT somewhere in the shadows keeps Marc
awake.

Linda whirls toward a KNOCK at her bedroom door.

Behind the curtain, CHILDREN are LAUGHING.
```

2.   **Type all *sound effects* that originate *onscreen* in all capital letters.** A sound effect, for purposes of this rule, is any natural, artificial or mechanical sound not produced live in front of the camera by an actor. This includes ticking clocks and nuclear explosions but *not* a woman's scream, so long as it originates onscreen in the lungs of a living, breathing actor.

```
Maverick quick-draws his SIX-SHOOTER and FIRES.

The laughing, screaming, shouting, giggling children
knock over the VASE, which SHATTERS on the bricks.

MUSIC PLAYS ON the old transistor RADIO.
```

Because they are sound effects, CAPITALIZE the following:

> Guns firing
> Bombs, grenades and fireworks exploding
> Bullets pinging and ricocheting
> Engines revving, idling, purring, roaring or dying
> Brakes grinding
> Tires squealing
> Horns honking
> Vehicles crashing
> Babies crying, burping or wailing (an effect because babies don't perform on cue)
> Animals growling, birds chirping (see "babies" above)
> Glass breaking or shattering
> Lumber splintering
> Radios, TVs, recorders, boom boxes, CD players and MP3 players playing
> Telephones and doorbells ringing
> Teletypes chattering
> Robots and computers beeping or clicking
> Teapots whistling
> Floors creaking
> Hinges squeaking

Water dripping, splashing, running, roaring or rushing
Waves crashing
Lightning cracking and thunder rumbling
Wind gusting, whistling or howling
Incorporeal beings speaking or moaning
Any sound that echoes, reverberates or fades away

Because they are natural sounds made live by actors, DON'T CAPITALIZE the following:

Onscreen characters laughing, talking, shouting, screaming, humming, singing, coughing, sneezing or wheezing.
Onscreen characters clapping their hands, snapping their fingers or tapping their pencils or toes.
Onscreen characters knocking on doors.
Onscreen crowds applauding, roaring, cheering the mayor or booing a dictator.
Onscreen musicians playing instruments.

3.   When capitalizing for sound effects and offscreen sounds, **always capitalize both the thing making the sound and the sound it makes.** For example, if a gun fires, type, "The GUN FIRES," because the gun is the thing making the sound and "fires" is the sound the gun makes. Other examples:

```
The CHERRY BOMB smokes silently for several long
seconds, then abruptly EXPLODES.

Gonzalez picks up the RINGING PHONE.

There's a flash of lightning, followed by the LOW RUMBLE
of THUNDER.

The executioner's FOOTSTEPS ECHO off the polished
floors.

Chuck turns ON the RADIO.  SCRATCHY JAZZ PLAYS.  He
snaps the RADIO back OFF.

The brawl overturns the JUKE BOX and the MUSIC COMES TO
a SCREECHING HALT.

The FIAT SQUEALS around the corner, ENGINE RACING,
DOWNSHIFTS and ROARS away up the street, TIRES
SCREAMING.

A BULLET SHATTERS the WINDOW and PINGS OFF the seat
belt.  The next BULLET RICOCHETS around the inside of
the car.  The third BULLET THUDS into Markie's chest.
```

```
SKYLARKS TWITTER in the morning air.  The BABY GURGLES
happily. The FLOOR CREAKS as Mary crosses to the
WHISTLING TEAPOT.  Her CELL PHONE RINGS "BROWN-EYED
GIRL."  And then all SOUND FADES SLOWLY to silence.
```

Capitalize the word "sound" only as a last resort, if there is nothing more specific to describe what is heard:

```
The children wake to the sound of a DISTANT MARCHING
BAND.
```

```
Somewhere in the bushes, Markie hears a SOFT SOUND.
```

Describing camera direction

The third and final reason for typing words in all capital letters in direction is because they provide camera direction. A single, three-part rule governs capitalization for camera direction: **Always capitalize 1) the word "camera"; 2) any movement the camera makes; and 3) any prepositions that relate to the camera or its movement.**

1.   Always capitalize the word "camera":

```
The horse gallops directly AT CAMERA.
```

This applies of course only when "camera" refers to the camera filming the movie, not to prop cameras *in* the movie:

```
The photographer swings his still camera round and round
over his head, then lets it fly PAST CAMERA.
```

If the words "we" or "us" are used in place of the word "camera," do not capitalize them:

```
We PASS ABOVE the battle and SWOOP INTO the clouds, a
flock of doves passing just BELOW us.
```

Never capitalize the phrase "we see":

```
We see a duck floating in the oily water.
```

It's a good idea to avoid using the formulation "we see." Instead of writing, "We see a duck floating in the oily water," write, "A duck floats in the oily water." It's more economical and avoids forcing the reader and writer onto the page in the form of "we."

2.   Capitalize any movement the camera makes (whether or not the word "camera" is actually used or is only implied):

CAMERA TRACKS Foster as he tumbles down the rocky slope.

As the jury enters, PAN their grim faces.

Winters climbs in the Volvo. RACK FOCUS TO Sommers
climbing out of the Saab.

Sailors pour onto the deck of the destroyer. TILT UP to
see Japanese Zeroes racing over their heads.

CAMERA MOVES WITH Englund ACROSS the trading floor.

As the roar of the unruly crowd builds, ZOOM IN ON young
Charlie, alone in the mob.

Shane stands in the center of Main Street. CRANE UP
until he looks very, very small.

HOLD ON Lamaster's face.

CAMERA FLIES LOW OVER the carnage on Omaha Beach during
the thick of the invasion.

3.   Capitalize any prepositions that relate to the camera or its movement. These may
     relate to the actual movement of the camera or to the movement of someone or
     something in relation to the camera:

CAMERA ROCKETS UP and UP and UP until it FLOATS ABOVE
the smoke of the burning city.

We FOLLOW Sylvia THROUGH the door, INTO the crowded
disco, UP the long stairway and ALONG a corridor, PAST a
beefy bouncer TOWARD a dying Muggeridge.

The balloon floats OVER CAMERA.

The runner sprints PAST us.

The biplane flies right AT us.

Lincoln sits facing the stage, his back TO CAMERA.

Adams turns TOWARD CAMERA.

The expressions "into frame," "out of frame," "into view" and "out of view"

The words "into frame" and "out of frame" represent camera direction and are always capitalized:

```
Waters steps INTO FRAME.  He lets out a high-pitched
laugh then immediately drops OUT OF FRAME.
```

The words "into view" and "out of view" are sometimes used interchangeably with "into frame" and "out of frame." When they are, they are capitalized:

```
Waters steps INTO VIEW.  He lets out a high-pitched
laugh then immediately drops OUT OF VIEW.
```

At other times, someone or something comes into view not because it has crossed the threshold of the camera's frame (making the words "into view" camera direction), but because it has emerged from behind something else. This is not camera direction and should not be capitalized:

```
Tired of playing hide-and-seek, Waters crawls into view
from his hiding place behind the couch.  Then he changes
his mind and hurries out of view behind the kitchen
door.
```

Freeze frame

The term *freeze frame* refers to an onscreen image that remains still, or frozen, for a period of time. When a moving image freezes midscene, the words "freeze frame" are placed in direction and typed in all capital letters:

```
Golda spots Sam across the tidy fence.  He's in his best
suit.  She's covered with mud from the garden.  His lips
curl into a tiny smile.  FREEZE FRAME.
```

If the shot consists of nothing but a still image from start to finish, the words "freeze frame" can appear in the shot heading:

```
FREEZE FRAME - HINDENBURG

At the precise instant flames engulf the airship.
```

A handful of exceptions to prove the rule

A few miscellaneous items that don't fit neatly into the above categories also get typed in all capital letters: *superimpositions*, the words "*ad lib,*" certain abbreviations and, optionally, the text of *signs, banners and headlines.*

Superimpositions

A superimposition occurs when words such as "One Year Later" appear on the screen. The word "superimpose" or just "super" is typed in all capital letters, followed by a colon and the words to be supered in all caps and quotation marks. The words can be set on a line by themselves and centered:

```
SUPERIMPOSE:


        "SOUTH CHINA SEA, 1938"
```

Or they can be embedded within a paragraph of direction:

```
A street car passes.  SUPER: "30 YEARS EARLIER."
```

Ad libs

When actors improvise dialogue, they are said to be speaking "ad lib." The words "ad lib" are always typed in all capital letters:

```
Joanie pops out of the giant cake.  Her grandparents AD
LIB their surprise.
```

Capitalized abbreviations

The abbreviations V.O. and O.S. are always typed in all caps, with periods. O.S. stands for offscreen, or outside the view of the camera. V.O. stands for voice over, which refers to the sound of a voice that originates from some location outside the current scene. In other words, someone standing just outside the frame could be heard speaking O.S. (i.e. from offscreen), while someone speaking by telephone from a location a continent away would only be heard speaking V.O. (i.e. voice over).

Signs, banners and headlines

The text of a sign, banner or headline may be typed in all capital letters, at the writer's discretion:

```
The sign at the front of the store reads, "HELP WANTED."
And below that, in letters not much smaller, "Japs Need
Not Apply."

The kids unfurl a scroll of paper written in bright
crayon.  "HAPPY BIRTHDAY, MISS BEASELY!"

Bobbie pages breathlessly through the paper until she
finds the article headlined: "'MIRACLE' SAVES GIRL AT
BURGER KING."
```

Capitalizing the first letter of direction following a shot heading

The first letter of direction following a shot heading should be capitalized unless the shot heading forms a complete sentence with the direction that follows it. Consider the following examples:

```
CLOSE ON MUSTANG CONVERTIBLE

As its emergency lights flash.

MAGGIE

Grimacing.  She'll never admit it but her shoulder is
killing her.

EXT. WATER TOWER - NIGHT

Lit up by a ring of floodlights below.
```

But:

```
JOSH

types an urgent command into the keyboard.  The
countdown stops.

CLOSE - CHIHUAHUA

scampers over the counters, lapping up the spilled beer.
```

What NOT to capitalize: EVERYTHING ELSE

If it doesn't fall into one of the above categories, don't type it in capital letters. Do not capitalize:

Props
Characters' actions
Visual effects
Lighting cues
Character names in direction if it isn't the first time they appear
Nonspeaking character names
The words "we see"
The word "silence"
The abbreviation "b.g." for background
The abbreviation "f.g." for foreground

Underscoring in direction

Underscoring, or underlining, may be used in direction for emphasis. Readers of scripts read swiftly and on occasion the judicious use of underscoring can help to ensure that an essential bit of information gets noticed or is given the necessary emphasis. A word of caution, though: Overuse of underscoring in direction looks amateurish and, like the boy who cried wolf, eventually gets ignored.

```
Maggie races up the steps toward the children's room.
She throws open the door and looks inside.

INT. CHILDREN'S BEDROOM

All three of the beds are empty.
```

Underscoring of multiple words is always continuous (not <u>All</u> <u>three</u> <u>of</u> <u>the</u> <u>beds</u> <u>are</u> <u>empty</u>). Notice also that the punctuation at the end of the sentence doesn't get underscored.

Breaking words with a hyphen in direction

Words in direction may be broken at the right margin of direction with a hyphen:

```
Radcliffe catches the ball in the air.  He's hit, pirou-
ettes on one foot, then falls.
```

Hyphenation is generally infrequent in scripts and should be used sparingly, only to avoid an unacceptably short line. In no case should two lines in a row be broken with hyphens.

Text messages and instant messages

When the content of text messages and instant messages must be shown onscreen, they can be included in direction. Simply describe them like any other visual element in the scene. Keep in mind that viewers prefer not to read large quantities of text in their movies and television episodes. The example below addresses this challenge by presenting only part of the electronic conversation in text, and the rest in voice-over dialogue.

```
INT. SINCLAIR KITCHEN - AFTERNOON

Jackie's cooking.  She's got her laptop open on the
counter.  Charlie's working on homework at the table.
Zoe breezes in and checks out the computer screen.
```

                          ZOE
          Hi, Mom. Whatcha doing?

She's logged onto UPS.com and is entering a string of
numbers.

                          JACKIE
          Tracking my new bed. You're
          going to love it. It's called a
          California king. It's huge.

There's a CUTE MUSICAL CHIME and an instant message
window pops up on her screen from someone named
"SLUGGER." Zoe reads the message:

                          ZOE
          "Hey, J-Bird, where ya been?"
                    (then)
          Who's Slugger?

Jackie casually turns the screen away from Zoe.

                          JACKIE
          Sit down. Get started on your
          homework.

Jackie tends to her cooking until Zoe sits and digs into
her books. Jackie quickly types:

          "J-BIRD: I have a life."

She hits enter. Goes about her cooking. The COMPUTER
CHIMES again almost instantly. Zoe glances up. Jackie
reads:

          "SLUGGER: Good. I like that in
          a girl."

Then a second line pops up, another CHIME:

          "SLUGGER: You make any decisions
          on where to put your new pool?"

Jackie mutes the computer. Casts a look at Zoe, then
types:

          "J-BIRD: Where do you stand on
          full sun versus partial shade?"

```
The answer comes back:

            "SLUGGER:  I like everything out
            in the open."

A second line appears, this time accompanied by a male
voice:

                    SLUGGER (V.O.)
            How about you?

Jackie thinks about that.  Types her reply:

                    JACKIE (V.O.)
            We still talking about pools?

                    SLUGGER (V.O.)
            Not necessarily.

Jackie thinks a little longer.  Steals a look at Zoe and
Charlie before typing:

                    JACKIE (V.O.)
            Okay.
```

Notice that the content of the text messages is set within dialogue margins for the sake of clarity, and to give the reader the sense of a conversation. This isn't the only way to format such a sequence, but it's one simple, clear and professional approach.

Caller ID

If the text displayed on a phone's caller ID needs to be shown on screen, it must be described in direction. You can do it like this:

```
Rabbit's new CORDLESS RINGS.  She dances over and plucks
it from its cradle with her unique brand of dizzy
panache.  She studies the caller ID and her face falls.

                    "PATTERSON, DICK
                    212-555-1542"

The PHONE KEEPS RINGING in Rabbit's hand.  She gingerly
replaces it in its cradle.  Drained of dizzy panache.
```

As an alternative, slightly less space is required by the following method.

> Rabbit's new CORDLESS RINGS. She dances over and plucks
> it from its cradle with her unique brand of dizzy
> panache. She studies the caller ID and her face falls.
> It reads: "PATTERSON, DICK, 212-555-1542."
>
> The PHONE KEEPS RINGING in Rabbit's hand. She gingerly
> replaces it in its cradle. Drained of dizzy panache.

Either of these approaches is clearer than the following, which comes across as sloppy and incomplete. Don't do this:

> Rabbit's new CORDLESS RINGS. She dances over and plucks
> it from its cradle with her unique brand of dizzy
> panache. Her face falls. It's Dick.
>
> The PHONE KEEPS RINGING in Rabbit's hand. She gingerly
> replaces it in its cradle. Drained of dizzy panache.

Here, the writer has failed to specify how the audience will know that it's Dick calling, and has left open the possibility that Rabbit has actually answered the phone. Strive always for clarity, and never leave readers confused.

Email

To indicate that the content of an email message should be shown on screen, the relevant text can be included in direction. Remember to write with economy, including the minimum text necessary in order to focus the reader's attention precisely where you want it.

If only a few words from an email message need to be displayed on screen, they can be formatted like this:

> Lt. Breaker leans sloppily on the keyboard, drunk. He
> squints at the computer screen, doing everything he can
> to focus on the words at the bottom of the email:
>
> "... Dixie never paid her share... "
>
> He lets out a little gasp. Because even in his current
> state, he understands what it means.

If the email's address or subject fields must be included, they can be written like this:

> Lt. Breaker leans sloppily on the keyboard, drunk. He
> squints at the computer screen. Clicks the mouse. An
> email message opens up.
>
> "From: Jacob Swimmer."

```
"Subject:  "Why I'm never gonna give you a dime."

Breaker squeezes his temples, doing everything he can to
focus on the words at the bottom of the email:

"... Dixie never paid her share... "

He lets out a little gasp.  Because even in his current
state, he understands what it means.
```

As always, the goal is brevity and clarity.

FAQs about direction

Is it true that a screenwriter should only describe what a character says and does, and that it's a mistake to write anything about what a character is thinking or feeling?

Because the camera doesn't typically go inside a character's head, the audience can't directly read a character's thoughts and feelings as they would in a novel. That's the reason for the advice you've heard. Describe what the audience can see and hear. If that instruction sounds terribly restrictive, consider that it might be broader than you might first think. I can see Tarzan swing on a vine. I can hear his jungle yell. But I can also see worry in his eyes. I can see realization dawn. I can even see him make a decision. The true limiting factor is how much thought and emotion an actor can meaningfully communicate through the camera's lens. Don't write, "Tarzan hangs from the vine, remembering the time he fell from a tree much like the one from which he now hangs and nearly died, troubled by the cruel irony that has brought him once again into mortal danger." You're asking too much of an actor. But do write, "Tarzan hangs from the vine, his eyes measuring the distance to the ledge. Can he make it?" I believe an actor can effectively convey that thought process. If it can be photographed, it's fair game. Put it on the page. Otherwise, leave it out.

I notice that your script samples use two spaces after each sentence, and that you advise writers to do the same. The publishing world has long since abandoned the two spaces after a period for one. Shouldn't we do the same with scripts?

Akiva Goldsman, a talented scribe responsible for writing not only some of the blockbuster Batman films but also *A Beautiful Mind*, insisted that the script processing folks at Warner Bros. use just one space after periods in his scripts. It drove the typists crazy because they were so used to hitting the space bar twice at the end of every sentence. In the end, we let the typists do what habit forced them to do, and we wrote a macro that replaced the two spaces with one. Akiva wasn't wrong. But many writers do continue to use two spaces between sentences. It makes sense because everyone who works in production has an interest in maintaining a reasonably regular number of characters per line, and lines per page, for timing and budgeting reasons. Changing the number of spaces between sentences tweaks that page count, however slightly. It's a small point. Bottom line: you're probably safe going with your own preference, one space or two. Unless you run across a curmudgeonly reader for whom that missing space has become a pet peeve.

Can you recommend a nice cabernet?

Justin Vineyard's 2005 Reserve Cabernet Sauvignon is an excellent example of the best red wines coming out of Paso Robles and is delicious.

How do I indicate cues for the film's score? I'm writing a thriller, and I know exactly where I want the music to come in to support the suspense of key scenes.

Don't do it. Step away from the keyboard. Pull on a pair of mittens before you do something you'll regret. The screenwriter doesn't write about the score. Doesn't mention the score. Doesn't know the score exists. Which means that screenwriters work at a disadvantage. Many of the elements that create emotion — like the score — or that make characters relatable — like the movie stars who play them — aren't available to the screenwriter. Your characters, and their dialogue and actions, must stand on their own. If that sounds like an absolute pronouncement, it is. And it comes with at least one obvious exception. If you're writing a spoof on horror films, an over-the-top musical sting might become a running gag, and it would certainly fall within the writer's jurisdiction to script such a thing.

Does the same thing apply to references to main and end titles?

Yep. Mittens. Unless you have a compelling reason to do otherwise. Why draw attention to the fact that we're reading a script? Let us get lost in imagining and experiencing the film without intrusions from the writer telling us that the credits have begun or ended. What difference does it make? Leave 'em out. Unless, as the fella said, you have a compelling reason to do otherwise.

DIALOGUE

Dialogue consists of three parts: 1) the name of the character who is speaking; 2) the words that are spoken; and 3) any parenthetical direction related to how the line is spoken or what the character is doing during the speech.

```
                        ¹LOUISE
                 ³(rifling her purse)
            ²Where did I put that check?
            Where is it?!
```

Character name over dialogue

The first and simplest rule here is that a character's name over dialogue should remain consistent throughout a script. With large numbers of speaking characters in a cast, this isn't always easy to achieve. The name of a character introduced as CAPTAIN MILFORD BROOKS shouldn't appear over dialogue first as CAPTAIN, later as CAPT. BROOKS, and later still as BROOKS. Choose one name for each character and use it consistently over dialogue.

Changing a character's name over dialogue

Sometimes, a character's name over dialogue *must* change. When that happens, it is done in a clear and orderly way. Say a character has been introduced as FEMALE SURGEON and that name appears over her dialogue:

```
    A FEMALE SURGEON strides into the operating room.

                        FEMALE SURGEON
            I'm going to need coffee, black,
            stat!  That plate of egg rolls
            from the lounge!  And a breath mint
            for the anesthesiologist!
```

Later, we learn the surgeon's name and decide to switch to using that name over dialogue. We do it like this:

```
                        SURGICAL NURSE
                (rolling his eyes)
            Good morning, Dr. Crump.

                        CRUMP (FEMALE SURGEON)
            'Morning, sunshine.
```

```
          Crump picks up a scalpel and goes to work.

                              CRUMP
                    Keep those breath mints coming.
```

The first time a character's new name appears over dialogue, the old name appears beside it in parentheses. From then on, the new name is used alone over dialogue. The change has been made in a way that confuses no one.

Numbered names over dialogue

A group of minor characters, say guards or doctors, may be introduced and have only a small number of lines. These characters sometimes never receive individual names like Sal or Throckmorton. They're simply Guard One, Guard Two and Guard Three. Or First Doctor, Second Doctor and Third Doctor. Or Assassin #1, Assassin #2 and Assassin #3. Any of these numbering schemes is acceptable. Simply be consistent:

```
                              ASSASSIN #1
                    Where are the bullets?


                              ASSASSIN #2
                    I thought you had the bullets!


                              ASSASSIN #3
                    We have no bullets?!
```

Group names over dialogue

Sometimes a group of characters speak together, all saying the same thing, and a plural or group name over dialogue is used:

```
          The MARINES respond in unison.

                              MARINES
                    Semper fi!
```

It is also possible to use a plural name over dialogue for a group of characters who speak simultaneous but distinct lines:

```
          REPORTERS swarm around the mayor.

                              REPORTERS
                    Mr. Mayor!/How do you respond to
                    the charges?/Will you have to
                    drop out of the campaign?/Do you
                    deny the allegations?
```

This is the simplest way to handle short bursts of simultaneous dialogue. A more involved method is described later, under the heading *Double, triple or quadruple dialogue.*

Capitalizing McDonald's and DeVries over dialogue

Just like with shot headings, when names like McDonald's and DeVries appear over dialogue, capitalize like this:

> McDONALD'S MANAGER
> C'mon, c'mon. Who's on registers?

> DeVRIES
> Ciao now, brown cow.

V.O. and O.S.: When we don't see the person talking

Often dialogue is spoken by characters who aren't visible onscreen at the time their voices are heard. When this happens, the abbreviation V.O. or O.S. appears beside the character name over dialogue. Where and when each designation applies has been a source of great confusion among writers. The rule is this: **When a character is physically present in a scene but is simply outside the view of the camera while speaking, he is offscreen and the abbreviation O.S. applies. The abbreviation V.O. applies in every other case**: voices heard over telephones, answering machines, tape recorders, TVs, loudspeakers and radios, the voices of narrators, voices that overlap from preceding or following scenes and voices originating in memory, imagination or hallucination. The abbreviations V.O. and O.S. appear beside the character name, capitalized, with periods, enclosed in parentheses.

> Melissa pushes play on her ANSWERING MACHINE. There's a
> BEEP, then:

> MRS. TEAGUE (V.O.)
> Melissa? Melissa, it's Mom. If
> you're there, pick up. Sweetheart,
> it's an emergency. Your daddy cut
> up all my plastic again.

> The sun rises over Walton's Mountain.

> NARRATOR (V.O.)
> That was the last time John Boy
> ever saw his uncle. But he never
> forgot the man. Or the lesson he
> had taught.

A TV behind the bar is PLAYING the NEWS:

                    NEWS ANCHOR (V.O.)
          ... Authorities say that the
          storm is expected to strike about
          midnight tonight.

Nick snaps up the RINGING PHONE.

                    NICK
          This is Nick.

                    MARY (V.O.)
               (on phone)
          It's me. I'm still waiting.

Jake tumbles through space, the helmet of his space suit
shattered, his face a mask of terror, as the space ship
drifts away from him.

                    MOM (V.O.)
          Jake. Wake up, Jake. You're going
          to miss the school bus.

INT. JAKE'S BEDROOM - MORNING

His eyes snap open and he looks up at his longsuffering
Mom. Gives her a queasy smile.

All of the above examples are designated V.O. because the voice comes from somewhere outside
the physical location of the scene. In the next example, the voice originates nearby, but outside
the view of the camera, and is therefore designated O.S.:

Queeg turns at the sound of Ned calling from outside the
locked door.

                    NED (O.S.)
          I'll break down this door, you
          don't open it. Don't think I
          won't.

Using "Voice" instead of V.O. and O.S.

An older, less common but still legitimate method of handling offscreen voices and voice overs is to use the word "voice" beside the unseen speaker's name:

> MARY'S VOICE
> (on phone)
> It's me. I'm still waiting.

> NED'S VOICE
> I'll break down this door,
> you don't open it. Don't think
> that I won't.

When this method is used, offscreen voices and voice overs are handled identically. Whichever method you decide to use, use it consistently throughout the script.

The words that are spoken

The actual words that characters speak comprise the vital heart of dialogue. Several guidelines apply. First, for the sake of the actors who will say them, **spell out every spoken word**. Instead of "Lt." type "Lieutenant." Instead of "St." type "Street." Or perhaps "Saint":

> ZUZU
> Lieutenant Gi lives on Saint
> Street.

Grammar, accents and colloquial speech

Characters speak in a manner consistent with who they are. Their grammar isn't always correct. Their sentences aren't always complete. They talk like real people talk. Consequently, incorrect grammar is common and acceptable in dialogue:

> SNAKE
> Ain't nobody gonna stop me.

Nonstandard spellings may be used when they serve to describe a unique way a character pronounces a word:

> AGENT GUTHRIE
> I plan to shoot that fat Eye-talian
> Al Capone.

> STEVE MARTIN
> Well excuuuuuuse me.

Accents can be suggested by judiciously modifying the spellings of words.

> TEX
> We're fixin' to do some dumpster
> divin'.

A strong word of caution here: When this sort of thing is overdone, it's murder to read. An accent can be suggested with word choices and syntax as well as spelling changes, and a little goes a very long way.

Emphasizing words in dialogue

To give a word or group of words in dialogue special force or emphasis, underscore them:

> MICAH
> Not this one. <u>That</u> one.

> SCHMIDT
> Go ahead. Call your New York
> lawyer. <u>We will bury you</u>.

As with underlining in direction, underscoring of multiple words is always continuous (not <u>We</u> <u>will</u> <u>bury</u> <u>you</u>). Notice also that the punctuation at the end of the sentence doesn't get underscored.

If you want to give even greater force to a word or group of words in dialogue, combine capitalization with the underscoring:

> SGT. LITTLE
> <u>Fire your weapons</u>! <u>FIRE</u>!!!

Don't use bold or italics. This rule dates to the era when scripts were typed on Underwoods and boldface and italic type weren't practical. It continues to make sense today because when an original print of a script is photocopied, as it will be if it's widely read, bold and italics can come to look more and more like regular type and the intended emphasis is lost.

Initials and acronyms in dialogue

Initials and acronyms occurring in dialogue should be typed in all capital letters. Initials are typed with periods to indicate to the actor that the letters are to be pronounced individually:

```
                    SCHRECKER
          We met at an I.E.P. for
          L.A.U.S.D.
```

Acronyms are typed without periods to indicate that they are to be pronounced as words:

```
                    SMYTHE
          He left FEMA to run an AIDS
          clinic.
```

This can be an extremely helpful pronunciation aid when the terms are technical and relatively unfamiliar:

```
                    DR. BECKETT
          Push the V-ZIG I.M. before the
          G.C.S.F., which is given sub-Q.
```

The above guidelines notwithstanding, some initials (e.g. TV and FBI) are so familiar that they present no risk of confusion even without periods and no harm is done if the periods are omitted.

Breaking words with a hyphen in dialogue

Unless the word is already hyphenated (e.g. sister-in-law), don't break words at the right margin of dialogue with a hyphen. Instead, move the entire word to the next line and keep it intact. Your actors will thank you. (A necessary exception occurs when a word is so long it can't possibly fit within the margins of dialogue. Sadly, very few such words actually exist.)

Parenthetical character direction

Parenthetical character direction refers to words of direction contained in parentheses within a line of dialogue:

```
                    JONAH
               (absolutely terrified)
          Why shouldn't you throw me
          overboard?
                    (eyeing the angry
                    water)
          I can't swim.  And I've a fear
          of fish.


                    SHIPMATE
          And we've a fear of drowning.
                    (looks at his fellow
                    sailors; smiles)
```

>   And there's more of us than
>   there are of you.

Five rules of parenthetical character direction

Five principle rules govern parenthetical character direction:

1. **Include in parenthetical direction only a description of how a line is spoken or what the character is doing while the line is being spoken.** Never include direction for anyone other than the character actually speaking. Never include technical direction such as sound effects or camera direction. All of the following are INCORRECT:

>   ALYSE
>   (Mike enters)
>   Hey, what's up?
>   (Mike ignores her)
>   Hell-o. Earth to Mike.

>   TREVOR
>   (PHONE RINGS)
>   Trevor Trotter speaking.

>   GRIFFIN
>   Stay right there.
>   (steps OUT OF FRAME,
>   returns)
>   I got you this book.

    All of what appears in parentheses above should be pulled out and placed in regular direction:

>   Mike enters.

>   ALYSE
>   Hey, what's up?

>   Mike ignores her.

>   ALYSE
>   Hell-o. Earth to Mike.

>   The PHONE RINGS.

>   TREVOR
>   Trevor Trotter speaking.

```
                    GRIFFIN
          Stay right there.


He steps OUT OF FRAME, returns.

                    GRIFFIN
          I got you this book.
```

2. **Never capitalize the first letter of parenthetical direction or add a period at the end.**
    Punctuation consists primarily of commas and semicolons, never a dash, never an ellipsis, and never a final period.

Instead of this:

```
                    HAMLET
          (Relishing the famous
           line.)
          To be or not to be.
```

Do this, lower-casing the first letter and omitting the final punctuation:

```
                    HAMLET
          (relishing the famous
           line)
          To be or not to be.
```

Instead of this:

```
                    NIXON
          (points to recorder...
           signals Haldeman to keep
           quiet -- smiles)
          I just had the new tape system
          installed.  Have to look out for my
          place in history, you know.
```

Do this, replacing the ellipsis and dash with semicolons:

```
                    NIXON
          (points to recorder;
           signals Haldeman to keep
           quiet; smiles)
          I just had the new tape system
          installed.  Have to look out for my
          place in history, you know.
```

As in the example above, multiple directions can be linked with semicolons:

>   SGT. SLICK
>   Hey, Jerry!
>   (waits a beat; throws
>   grenade; ducks)
>   Catch this.

A colon is also sometimes used:

>   CENSUS WORKER
>   (re: clipboard)
>   Sign here.

On rare occasions a question mark or exclamation point is used:

>   DEFENDANT
>   (gulp!)
>   I'd love to have dinner with
>   you, Your Honor.

>   SHEILA
>   (what, me worry?)
>   Bring it on.

3.   **Don't start parenthetical direction with "he" or "she." It's understood.**

Instead of this:

>   SHERIFF
>   (he draws his gun)
>   Stop right there.

Do this:

>   SHERIFF
>   (draws his gun)
>   Stop right there.

4.   **Don't let parenthetical direction run to more than four lines.**

Instead of this:

>   ROBBIE
>   Let me show you something.
>   (opens drawer, pulls
>   out three brightly

```
                        colored balls and
                        starts to juggle;
                        drops one and starts
                        again; a little
                        embarrassed)
              I'm still learning.
```

Do this:

```
                        ROBBIE
              Let me show you something.

    He opens a drawer, pulls out three brightly colored
    balls and starts to juggle.  He drops one and starts
    again.

                        ROBBIE
                  (a little embarrassed)
              I'm still learning.
```

5. **Don't place parenthetical direction at the end of a speech.**

Instead of this:

```
                        JOJO
                    (laughing)
              Don't you just wish.
                   (touches his arm)
```

Do this:

```
                        JOJO
                    (laughing)
              Don't you just wish.

    She touches his arm.
```

An important exception to this rule, as writer John August has pointed out, occurs in scripts for animation, where speeches commonly end in parenthetical directions like "(sigh)" and "(nervous laugh)."

Sotto voce, beat, re:

Three terms get heavy use in parenthetical direction: *sotto voce*, *beat* and *re:*.

Sotto voce is Italian for "soft voice" and is used in parenthetical direction to instruct an actor to deliver a line quietly or under his breath:

```
                    PRESIDENTIAL CANDIDATE
          I can't tell you how happy I am
          to be in North Dakota today.
                    (fake smile; sotto voce)
          Because I'm not.
```

Sotto voce is sometimes shortened to just "sotto":

```
                    BURGLAR
               (sotto)
          Hand me that crowbar.
```

A beat is a script term meaning a short pause. It appears often in both direction and parenthetical character direction:

```
                    NICHOLS
          Let's walk.
               (beat)
          On second thought, let's ride.
```

Beats come in several flavors:

```
                    SAMPSON
               (short beat)
          Why not?
```

```
                    DELILAH
               (long beat; shakes
                her head)
          We're dead.
```

```
                    RUNNING HORSE
          Know what I think?
               (two full beats;
                grins)
          Hell, I don't even know what I
          think.
```

```
                    Z
               (half a beat too
                slow)
          Of course I love you.
```

The term "re:" appears often in parenthetical direction, meaning "with regard to":

```
                      WHITE
              (re: his haircut)
         What d'ya think?
```

Foreign language dialogue and subtitles

When dialogue is in a foreign language, it can be written in the desired language, like this:

```
                    LARS OLE
         Hvor er du, Hans?
```

If you want the foreign dialogue to be subtitled, indicate that in parenthetical direction, in lower case letters, then type the dialogue in English, saving yourself years of foreign language study:

```
                    LARS OLE
              (in Norwegian;
               subtitled)
         Where are you, Hans?
```

If an entire conversation is subtitled, that can be indicated in direction, in all caps, preceding the exchange:

```
   The men speak in German with SUBTITLES:


                    HELMUT
         Have you ever seen a U-boat?


                    WERNER
         Never.  But isn't that the whole
         idea?
```

Song lyrics in dialogue

Unless the movie is a musical, type the song lyrics in upper and lower case letters, enclosed in quotation marks. Observe the lyrical line endings by wrapping the ends of long lines and indenting the wrapped text two spaces:

```
                      TEX
         "Home, home on the range
         Where the deer and the antelope play
         Where seldom is heard a discouraging
           word
```

>   And the skies are not cloudy all
>   day."

If the movie *is* a musical, type song lyrics in all capital letters, without quotation marks or ending punctuation:

>   TEX
>   HOME, HOME ON THE RANGE
>   WHERE THE DEER AND THE ANTELOPE PLAY
>   WHERE SELDOM IS HEARD A DISCOURAGING
>   WORD
>   AND THE SKIES ARE NOT CLOUDY ALL
>   DAY

Breaking a page in the middle of dialogue

Never break a page in the middle of a sentence in dialogue. Always split the page between sentences, add (MORE) at the bottom of the page, and (CONT'D) beside the character name at the top of the following page:

>   FRANCONI
>   The treatment lasts just over
>   a year.
>   (MORE)
>   -----page break -----
>   FRANCONI (CONT'D)
>   It starts with fractionated
>   radiotherapy combined with a
>   chemotherapeutic agent.

Not:

>   FRANCONI
>   The treatment lasts just over
>   a year. It starts with
>   (MORE)
>   -----page break -----
>   FRANCONI (CONT'D)
>   fractionated radiotherapy
>   combined with a chemotherapeutic
>   agent.

Never break dialogue with parenthetical direction at the bottom of the page. Instead, carry the parenthetical direction to the top of the following page, like this:

94

```
                         FRANCONI
          Vincristine.  It's given outpatient.
          Intravenously.
                         (MORE)
     -----page break -----
                         FRANCONI (CONT'D)
             (writing it down)
          Vincristine.  Look up the side
          effects.
```

Not:

```
                         FRANCONI
          Vincristine.  It's given outpatient.
          Intravenously.
                  (writing it down)
                         (MORE)
     -----page break -----
                         FRANCONI (CONT'D)
          Vincristine.  Look up the side
          effects.
```

Adding (cont'd), (CONT'D) or (continuing) when a speech is broken by direction

In years past, it was customary when a character's speech resumed after being broken by direction to indicate that it was a continuing speech. This was accomplished by adding (cont'd) or (CONT'D) beside the character name or the word "continuing" in parenthetical direction beneath the character name. It was done like this:

```
                         JONESY
          Come in.  Sit down.

     The PHONE RINGS.

                         JONESY (CONT'D)
          I'll get that.
```

Or:

```
                         JONESY
          Come in.  Sit down.

     The PHONE RINGS.
```

95

> JONESY (cont'd)
> I'll get that.

Or:

> JONESY
> Come in. Sit down.

The PHONE RINGS.

> JONESY
> (continuing)
> Come in. Sit down.

In each case, the determining factor was that the same character was continuing to speak, direction notwithstanding, without an intervening speech by another character.

Marking continuing speeches ceased to be standard practice in Hollywood in the 1980s. The practice made a resurgence years later, with the advent of script software that, through a programming quirk, defaulted to include (cont'd) beside the character name.

Writers now have a choice. If your script software is set to add (cont'd) or (CONT'D) or (continuing) when a speech is broken by direction, you can leave it that way because readers are accustomed to seeing it. You can also feel free to turn it off. I prefer to omit (cont'd) beside the character name in order to save words and streamline my scripts.

(**An important caveat**: The one place the inclusion of (CONT'D) beside the character name remains mandatory is in multi-camera television format.)

Double, triple and quadruple dialogue

As a more flexible alternative to group dialogue, as described earlier, when multiple characters speak at the same time their dialogue can be typed in side-by-side columns like this:

SLADKEY	BROWN
I told him but he didn't	I told you exactly what
listen. He never	to say. I told you
listens.	what to do if he didn't
(not listening)	listen. Why don't you
What do you want me to	ever listen?
do?	

Complete, separate conversations can run in parallel columns:

```
        SLADKEY                        LISZT
Is Manny there?              I'm calling from Doctor
                            Brockman's office.

      MARIA (V.O.)
He's at the mill.                 JUNE (V.O.)
                            Are my results back?

        SLADKEY
Really?  I thought he was           LISZT
working nights now.         Not yet.  There was a
                            mix-up at the lab.  We
      MARIA (V.O.)          need you to come back
He's filling in for         for another blood draw.
someone out sick.
                                  JUNE (V.O.)
        SLADKEY             Ah no.  You're kidding
Tell him I called.          me.
```

Two, three, four and even five characters can speak simultaneously:

```
                        SLADKEY
                Kids, I'm home.  Who wants
                pizza?


    RACHEL              HOPE              PETER
Where's it from?    I want sausage.   I'm not hungry.


Sladkey opens the box on the counter.


                        SLADKEY
                Just get in here.  I got
                pepperoni.


  RACHEL            HOPE            PETER            EMILY
From where?     Not sausage?    I'm not hungry!  Yeah!!!


                      SLADKEY
                Where's Pam?


Pam enters from the bathroom.


    PAM        RACHEL        HOPE        PETER         EMILY
Here I am!   Pam who?    Pam hates    Pam owes     Yeah, Pam!!!
                        pizza.       me five
                                     dollars!
```

Bear in mind that simultaneous dialogue can be tedious to read and should be used sparingly.

97

Margins for simultaneous dialogue

Margins for simultaneous dialogue are as follows:

Two simultaneous speakers

1. **Dialogue**
    First speaker
    Left margin is 1.9"
    Right margin is 4.5"
    Second speaker
    Left margin is 4.0"
    Right margin is 2.0"

2. **Character name over dialogue**
    First speaker
    Left margin is 2.7"
    Second speaker
    Left margin is 5.2"

Three simultaneous speakers

1. **Dialogue**
    First speaker
    Left margin is 1.7"
    Right margin is 5.3"
    Second speaker
    Left margin is 3.5"
    Right margin is 3.5"
    Third speaker
    Left margin is 5.3"
    Right margin is 1.7"

2. **Character name over dialogue**
    First speaker
    Left margin is 2.2"
    Second speaker
    Left margin is 4.0"
    Third speaker
    Left margin is 5.8"

Four simultaneous speakers

1.   Dialogue
First speaker
Left margin is 1.6"
Right margin is 5.8"
Second speaker
Left margin is 3.0"
Right margin is 4.4"
Third speaker
Left margin is 4.4"
Right margin is 3.0"
Fourth speaker
Left margin is 5.8"
Right margin is 1.6"

2.   Character name over dialogue
First speaker
Left margin is 1.9"
Second speaker
Left margin is 3.3"
Third speaker
Left margin is 4.7"
Fourth speaker
Left margin is 6.1"

FAQs about dialogue

Don't actors hate parenthetical character directions? Don't they just sit down with their script and cross them all out?

Um, no. But you'll hear absolute pronouncements to that effect. The truth is that professional writers use parentheticals all the time. John Wells, former president of the Writers Guild of America West and the show runner behind the series *China Beach*, *ER*, *Third Watch*, and, in its later seasons, *The West Wing*, is a prolific user of parentheticals. But he doesn't use them to give actors instructions about how to deliver their lines, obvious things like "(angrily)" or "(brooding)." Instead, he uses parentheticals like "(and)" and "(then)" for rhythm and pacing, to break up longer speeches into their discrete emotional movements. He uses them like a poet uses line length.

Consider the way parentheticals are used in the following passage:

```
EXT. MOUNTAIN FIRE ROAD - DAY

Jackie and Sylvia hike along a ridge above Malibu.
```

                    SYLVIA
          He wants to meet? Where?

                    JACKIE
          A restaurant up in the Valley.

                    SYLVIA
          Are you going to do it?

                    JACKIE
          No!
                    (then)
          I don't know.
                    (then)
          Should I?

                    SYLVIA
          Well. Where do you want this
          thing to go?

                    JACKIE
          What do you mean?

                    SYLVIA
          I mean, are you really that
          unhappy with David?

Jackie stops walking. She drinks from a water bottle
and looks out toward the Pacific.

                    JACKIE
          I'm not going to leave him. I'll
          never do that to my kids.

                    SYLVIA
          Till death do you part.
                    (beat)
          So what are you looking for here?

                    JACKIE
          Oh God, Sylvia, it feels so good
          to be talking to a man at this
          level again. I've been so alone
          for so long and I didn't even
          know it.
                    (beat)

>   Couldn't it be better for
>   everyone? If I could be happy
>   like that again?
>
>   SYLVIA
>   (takes a long drink)
>   Know what I think?
>   (wicked smile)
>   You should just run off with this
>   guy. And I'll move into your
>   house and take over your life.

Legitimate uses of parenthetical character direction include:

- to break up a long speech visually, or for the purposes of pacing
- to clarify the feeling with which a line is spoken when it's not apparent from the context, or when it's the opposite of what would otherwise be expected
- to describe an action a character takes in the midst of a speech

No actor is likely to cross out parenthetical direction of this kind.

Do you know anyone named Fred?

Yes.

I want the audience to hear the dialogue from a scene before we actually cut to the scene. I think it's called a pre-lap voice over. How do I do that?

Like this:

>   EXT. SINCLAIR HOUSE — NIGHT
>
>   A strange, impossible view. The CAMERA FLOATS bizarrely
>   ABOVE the Sinclair house, LOOKING DOWN as if from a
>   dream. The quiet is broken by a CHILD'S CRY.
>
>   CHARLIE (V.O.)
>   I know it was a dream but --
>
>
>   INT. CHARLIE'S BEDROOM - NIGHT
>
>   A sleepy Zoe sits on the bed rubbing Charlie's back. He
>   looks at Jackie with eyes filled with fear.

> CHARLIE
> Don't you remember last summer
> when I dreamed Whisper died --
> then he got hit by a car?

Was that you that day in Helsinki?

Possibly. Was that you?

TRANSITIONS

Transitions are the various methods by which one shot or scene changes to the next. They include *cuts*, *dissolves*, *fades* and *wipes*:

```
FADE IN:

THREE GIANT PUMPKINS

baking under a Texas sun.

                                        DISSOLVE TO:

LITTLE BOY

Striking a match.

                                        CUT TO:

SCARECROW

Burning brightly.   The boy watches.

                                        WIPE TO:

300-POUND FARMER

has the boy by the ear, dragging him toward the
woodshed.

                                        FADE OUT.
```

With the exception of FADE IN, all transitions are typed 6.0" from the left edge of the page.

Fades

A *fade in* is a gradual transition from a solid color, usually black, to a filmed image. A *fade out* is the reverse, a gradual transition from a filmed image to black. FADE IN: is typed at the left margin for direction in all capital letters, followed by a colon:

```
FADE IN:
```

FADE OUT. is typed 6.0" from the left edge of the page in all capital letters followed by a period:

FADE OUT.

Feature film scripts usually begin with a FADE IN: and end with a FADE OUT., but they don't necessarily have to.

Television scripts are usually divided by several act breaks representing commercial breaks, and each act typically begins with a FADE IN: and ends with a FADE OUT.

FADE TO BLACK can be used as an alternative to FADE OUT:

FADE TO BLACK.

When a transition consists of a fade from a filmed image to a white screen write, "FADE TO WHITE":

FADE TO WHITE.

Cuts

The cut, an instantaneous shift from one shot to the next, is the most common transition:

CUT TO:

When no transition is indicated, a cut is assumed. An entire script can actually be written without any transitions being indicated at all and the reader will assume that every transition is a cut.

Why then would a writer ever specify a cut?

Some writers use "CUT TO" to establish a sense of rhythm or pace by placing a CUT TO: after every shot in an action sequence. A CUT TO: also creates white space on a page that might otherwise look too dense. And a CUT TO: added at the end of a sequence can give a heightened sense of finality, a more distinct sense that one thing has ended and a new thing has begun.

Note that CUT TO: is typed in all capital letters and followed by a colon.

Cuts come in various flavors, including the *hard cut*, which describes a transition that is jarring:

Jenny smells the rose.

HARD CUT TO:

SCREAMING LOCOMOTIVE

bearing down on her.

104

The *quick cut* is not one that happens faster than any other, but one that happens *sooner* than it otherwise might:

```
And just as Jason turns toward the blinding light --

                                            QUICK CUT TO:
```

A *time cut* emphasizes that time is passing from one shot to the next:

```
Far above the surf, Sweeney dozes on dry sand.

                                            TIME CUT TO:

SAME SCENE - TWO HOURS LATER

A wave washes over Sweeney and wakes him, sputtering.  The
tide has come in.
```

A *match cut* specifies a cut in which the image in the first shot either visually or thematically matches the image in the following shot:

```
The fat lady opens her mouth to sing.

                                            MATCH CUT TO:

LITTLE SALLY SALTER

Screaming like a banshee.
```

A *cut to black* (or white or any other color) can be used in lieu of a fade to black for dramatic effect, and is followed by a period:

```
Dr. Drake positions the bone saw over Jimmy's leg.

                                            CUT TO BLACK.
```

Dissolves

A dissolve is a gradual transition from one image to another. It often implies a passage of time:

```
Sister Margaret sits down outside the courtroom to wait.

                                            DISSOLVE TO:

INT. COURTHOUSE - LATER
```

Hours have passed and Sister Margaret is still here, still waiting.

Like cuts, dissolves come in a variety of flavors. There are slow dissolves, fast dissolves and the wavy effect known as a ripple dissolve, often used to suggest a transition into daydream or imagination:

Slim sits in his wheelchair and stares at the horse.

                              RIPPLE DISSOLVE TO:

HEAVENLY PASTURE

Slim rides at a full gallop, like the cowboy he once was.

If the transition is so long that it extends beyond the right margin and wraps to a second line, back it up so that it all fits on one line:

Josh and Heather stand hand in hand on the beach, staring out to sea.

                         UNBELIEVABLY SLOW DISSOLVE TO:

SUNSET OVER PACIFIC

Wipes

A wipe is a stylized transition in which the new image slides, or wipes, over the top of the old one:

BATMAN AND ROBIN

leap into the Batmobile. TIRES SPIN, flame spews -

                                   WIPE TO:

EXT. GOTHAM CITY POLICE HQ - DAY

The BATMOBILE SKIDS to a stop and the dynamic duo dismounts.

Breaking a page at a transition

When breaking a page at a transition, always break *after* the transition, not before. If the transition must be moved to the following page, some part of the preceding scene must go with it. With the exception of FADE IN, **a page must never begin with a transition**.

PUNCTUATION

The subject of punctuation in scripts merits special attention.

Period

A *period* at the end of a sentence is always followed by two spaces. However, a period that is part of the abbreviation EXT. or INT. in a shot heading is followed by just one space:

```
EXT. DESTROYER
```

Ellipsis

An *ellipsis* is three periods followed by a single space. It is most commonly used in dialogue to indicate that a character's speech has trailed off, many times before starting again:

```
                    MARVIN
          I'd like to say I'll help you but
          I just... I don't know.
```

An ellipsis is also used when we join a character midspeech:

```
                    NEWS ANCHOR (V.O.)
          ... Severe weather moving toward
          Wyandotte County with strong winds.
```

Ellipses are sometimes grossly overused. If a comma will suffice, use a comma. Reserve the ellipsis for its specialized uses.

Dash

A *dash* is two hyphens in sequence, with a space before and a space after. It is used in both dialogue and direction to set off parenthetical material:

```
          He's wearing a floppy hat -- the kind worn by Norwegian
          fishermen -- and staggering around like a serious drunk.
```

It is also used when dialogue abruptly breaks off:

```
                    HELGE
          What the --
```

Never leave a dash dangling on a line by itself:

```
                    PATSY
          Why anyone would say that is beyond
          --
```

Instead, carry the last word onto the line with the dash:

```
                    PATSY
          Why anyone would say that is
          beyond --
```

Hyphen

In scripts, the *hyphen* is used in the ordinary way, to hyphenate words like mother-in-law and three-year-old, and to break longer words at the ends of lines of direction:

```
    Teddy races toward the tracks, trying to beat the loco-
    motive to the crossing.
```

Use moderation when hyphenating at the ends of lines of *direction*, and never hyphenate the ends of two lines in a row.

Don't hyphenate words at the ends of lines of *dialogue* (unless they're already hyphenated, like writer-director). Instead of this:

```
                    DR. MATHIS
          Based on the imaging today, medullo-
          blastoma is a possibility.
```

Do this:

```
                    DR. MATHIS
          Based on the imaging today,
          medulloblastoma is a possibility.
```

The hyphen gets special treatment in shot headings. When used to separate elements in shot headings, the hyphen is sandwiched between two spaces, one before and one after:

```
    CLOSE SHOT - CLAW HAMMER
```

Hyphenate compound words when they are used like this:

```
    The horse is a two-year-old.  She's a two-year-old horse.
```

110

But not when they are used like this:

```
The horse is two years old.
```

Quotation marks

Quotation marks are placed around all quoted material, plus titles of:

> songs
> poems
> short stories
> television series
> newspaper articles
> magazine articles

Periods and commas always go *inside* the quotation marks:

```
On the monitors, reruns are playing of "Gilligan's Island,"
"The Beverly Hillbillies" and "Leave it to Beaver."
```

Semicolons and colons always go *outside* quotation marks:

```
Simon hums "Clementine"; Trevino pens the names of what he
calls "my boys": Johnny Walker and Jack Daniels.
```

Question marks and exclamation points go *inside* quotation marks when they are part of the original quotation:

```
The banner at the front of the church reads, "Hallelujah!"
```

```
Griffin laughs too loud at the "Got Milk?" commercial.
```

Question marks and exclamation points go *outside* when they are *not* part of the original quotation:

```
The horse leaps through the flames while the rider whistles
"The William Tell Overture"!
```

```
Who could have guessed he'd need to know the words of
Frost's "The Road Not Taken"?
```

Underscoring

Underscoring of multiple words is always continuous and the punctuation at the end of the sentence is not underscored. It should look like this:

111

        The money is gone.

Not this:

        The money is gone.

And not this:

        The money is gone.

Underscore:

        Names of ships
        Names of spacecraft
        Names of planes
        Book titles
        Magazine titles
        Newspaper titles
        Movie titles
        Play titles

        Spread on the desk are a copy of the Times, Milton's
        Paradise Lost, and Hamlet, plus books about the bomber
        Enola Gay and the destroyer Madison.

Punctuation and capitalization in direct address

Direct address refers to occasions in dialogue when a character uses the name of the person he is directly speaking to, or addressing. **Always set a name used in direct address apart with commas**:

                    SAL
        Hi, Deb. How's it going, Marge?
        Nikki, you mind passing the peas?

Plus, just as you would capitalize the first letter of a proper name, capitalize the first letter of any name used *in place of* a proper name in direct address:

                    WILLIAM
              (greeting his guests)
        Hello, Dad. Hi, Mom. How are
        you, Coach? Nice to see you,
        Sarge. You too, Officer. And,
        Your Honor, wow, what an honor!

112

But don't capitalize *pet names*, *terms of endearment* and the like:

```
                    WILLIAM
          It was a great party, honey.   I
          mean it, sweetheart.
                    (to tipsy guest)
          Time to head home, pal.
```

And don't capitalize improper names (e.g. mom, coach, sergeant) when they aren't being used in direct address:

```
                    WILLIAM
          What a party!   My dad was there.
          So was my mom and my high school
          track coach and my old drill
          sergeant and Judge Lemon and that
          nice police officer who looks
          like Carl Malden.
```

The first draft of a script can look different from a production draft in two important ways: the absence or presence of scene numbers and the absence or presence of CONTINUEDs at the tops and bottoms of pages.

CONTINUEDs at the tops and bottoms of pages

When a scene continues from one page to the next, a production draft includes the word (CONTINUED) at the bottom of the first page and the word CONTINUED: at the top of the second page.

> (CONTINUED) is double-spaced down from the last line of text and begins 6.0" from the left paper edge. It is typed in all capital letters, inside parentheses.

> CONTINUED: is double-spaced down from the page number and begins 1.7" from the left paper edge. It is typed in all capital letters and is followed by a colon.

A page broken with CONTINUEDs looks like this:

```
EXT. BATTLEFIELD - DAWN

The sun rises crimson over the fallen soldiers.  Ragged
children move among the dead, searching for survivors.
Or a serviceable pair of boots.

                                        (CONTINUED)
```

```
                                                      21.


CONTINUED:

                          UNION CAPTAIN
            You younguns, git!
                  (turning to his
                   men)
            Ever'body knows his job.  Let's
            git to it!
```

```
              The men start reluctantly across the field.

                                                 CUT TO:
```

Only use CONTINUEDs when a scene is broken between pages. When a scene ends at the bottom of a page and a new scene begins at the top of the following page, don't add CONTINUEDs:

```
              INT. CLOSET - DAY

              Schmidt listens as the FOOTSTEPS RECEDE.  He turns the
              handle and pushes open the closet door.
```

```
                                                          35.


              INT. HALLWAY - DAY

              Schmidt pokes his head into the hall and looks both ways.
              Sees the coast is clear.  He steps into the hall.
```

A script may use CONTINUEDs at any stage, but standard format *requires* that they be used when scene numbers are added.

Adding CONTINUEDs at the tops and bottoms of pages takes away space that would otherwise be filled by script content. Consequently, the page count increases when CONTINUEDs are added, usually by about 11%.

Scene numbers

Only a script that has reached preproduction should have *scene numbers*. Prior to preproduction, a script should not have scene numbers.

When scene numbers are added to a script, scenes are numbered consecutively beginning at 1, and every shot heading receives a number. (An alternative but less common method numbers only the master scene headings, those that move the action to a new location or a new period of time.)

Scene numbers are typed on both the left and right sides of the shot heading, like this:

```
22       EXT. GRANT'S HEADQUARTERS - NIGHT                       22
```

The left scene number begins 1.0" from the left paper edge.

The right scene number begins 7.4" from the left paper edge.

If a shot heading wraps onto a second line, the scene numbers remain on the first line:

```
9        EXT. NEW YORK CITY - CENTRAL PARK - WIDE ANGLE - BALL   9
         FIELD - DAY
```

When a scene continues from one page to the next, the scene numbers are placed on the same line as the CONTINUED:

```
121      EXT. BATTLEFIELD - DAWN                                121

         The sun rises crimson over the fallen soldiers.  Ragged
         children move among the dead, searching for survivors.
         Or a serviceable pair of boots.

                                      (CONTINUED)
```

```
                                                       109.


121    CONTINUED:                                        121

                          UNION CAPTAIN
                    You younguns, git!
```

If the above scene which begins on page 108 and continues on page 109 is long enough to extend onto page 110, a (2) is placed inside parentheses beside the CONTINUED on page 110:

```
                                                       110.


121    CONTINUED: (2)                                     121

                          SERGEANT
                    Gather those guns right here.
```

Don't be confused. Even though page 110 is the third page of the scene, it is the second CONTINUED page of the scene, and therefore gets a (2).

If the scene kept going, page 111 would get a CONTINUED: (3) and page 112 would get a CONTINUED: (4), and so on until there is a new scene with a new scene number.

When scene numbers are locked

As a script moves through preproduction it is eventually *boarded*, that is a production board is made up based on the scene numbers. Before a script is boarded, it is proper to renumber the scenes when changes are made that add or omit scenes. But after a script is boarded, the scene numbers are locked and shouldn't be changed. Production personnel are working based on the scene numbers that existed at the time the script was boarded.

Omitted scenes

If a scene in a locked script is omitted, it should be indicated as follows:

```
121     OMITTED                                         121


122     INT. GRANT'S TENT - NIGHT                       122

        Officers have gathered to await word from the general.
```

In that way, all scene numbers are accounted for and there is no uncertainty about what became of scene 121.

If two scenes are omitted, indicate the omission like this:

```
120     OMITTED                                         120
&                                                       &
121                                                     121


122     INT. GRANT'S TENT - NIGHT                       122

        Officers have gathered to await word from the general.
```

If a group of more than two scenes is omitted, indicate the omission as follows:

```
118     OMITTED                                         118
thru                                                    thru
121                                                     121


122     INT. GRANT'S TENT - NIGHT                       122

        Officers have gathered to await word from the general.
```

Numbering "A" scenes

If a new scene is added in a locked script, it is given a new, unique number, in this case 121A:

```
121     OMITTED                                                    121


121A    EXT. NIGHT SKY                                             121A

        Clouds cover the full moon.


122     INT. GRANT'S TENT - NIGHT                                  122

        Officers have gathered to await word from Grant.
```

If two or more scenes had been added, they would be numbered 121A, 121B, 121C, and so on. In rare instances more than 26 scenes are inserted and the whole alphabet is expended. When that happens, scene 121Z is followed by 121AA, 121BB, 121CC, and so on.

Add a hyphen to scenes lettered with an I or an O so that the letters aren't confused with numbers:

```
121-I   OMITTED                                                    121-I
thru                                                               thru
121-O                                                              121-O
```

If a new scene is added at some later date between scenes 121 and 121A, it is numbered A121A:

```
121     OMITTED                                                    121


A121A   ANGLE ON CAMPFIRE                                          A121A

        Sparks fly up.


121A    EXT. NIGHT SKY                                             121A

        Clouds cover the full moon.


122     INT. GRANT'S TENT - NIGHT                                  122

        Officers have gathered to await word from the general.
```

119

If two or more scenes had been added, they would be numbered A121A, B121A, C121A, and so on.

The principle is that scene A1 precedes scene 1 and scene 1A follows scene 1.

Colored paper

The first time a script receives wide distribution to production personnel, the pages are white. Subsequent versions of the script are distributed on colored paper to avoid the confusion of people working from different versions of the same script. The director can say, "Do you have the buff draft?" and the star can answer, "Buff? I'm still working from the green draft."

In the United States, the standard progression of colors is:

> white
> blue
> pink
> yellow
> green
> goldenrod
> buff
> salmon
> cherry
> tan

After tan the cycle repeats, starting over with white. Overseas productions often include other paper colors.

Revision marks

Once a script has received wide distribution, subsequent versions of the script should contain *revision marks* to help production personnel quickly locate the changes. The revision marks go in the right margin beside each line that contains changes, 7.8" from the left edge of the page. The most common revision mark is the *asterisk*:

```
121    OMITTED                                          121


121A   ANGLE ON CAMPFIRE                                121A  *

       Sparks fly up.                                         *


121B   EXT. NIGHT SKY                                   121B  *

       Clouds cover the full moon.                            *
```

122   INT. GRANT'S TENT - NIGHT   122

Officers have gathered to await word from the general.

If there are so many changes on a given page that more than ten asterisks would be required, a single asterisk goes at the top of the page, to the right of the page number:

---

                          110.   *

121   CONTINUED: (2)   121

                  SERGEANT
         Gather those guns right here.

Full drafts vs. revised pages

Many times, after a script has already received wide distribution to production personnel, extensive changes are made involving more than half the pages in the script and a whole new, full draft is issued. When this happens, the script is *repaginated.* That is, pages are renumbered with text moving up to fill in the space where omissions are made, and text moving down to make room for added material.

At other times, only a few pages are changed and only those *revised pages* (also called simply *revisions*) are issued. In this case, if a page has no changes, it isn't reprinted. Production personnel replace just the changed pages in their existing scripts. Not only does this practice save paper and expense, it preserves much of the current script and all of the many handwritten notes that frequently cover the pages of a script in preproduction or production.

Say there's a change on page 7 of a full draft of a script that was distributed on blue paper. The change is typed **with revisions marks indicating the location of changes**, the new page 7 is printed on the next color of paper, pink, and distributed. Recipients pull the old blue page 7 out of their scripts and put the new pink page 7 in its place.

In practice, of course, a set of revisions may involve 40 or 50 or even 60 revised pages. The principle, though, remains the same. The old pages are pulled out and the new pages are put in their place. The process of issuing revised pages frequently continues until the script contains every possible color of paper and is accurately described as a *rainbow script.*

Revision slugs

Every page of a set of revised pages bears a *revision slug* at the top of the page, on the same line as the page number, that includes the title (in all capital letters) and date of the revisions:

```
UNDER THE TABLE - Rev. 3/11/09                          17.
```

For series television, include both the series title (all caps) and episode title (upper and lower case with quotation marks), plus the revision date:

```
ALIAS - "A Life Apart" - Rev. 2/21/04                   59.
```

The revision slug begins 1.7" from the left edge of the page.

Deleting material from revised pages

If material is deleted from a page, that page remains short. In the following example, scene 23 is being omitted from page 12 of a script titled *Grant* in a set of revisions dated 1/1/04:

```
GRANT - Rev. 1/1/04 12.

22 EXT. TENT - NIGHT      22

   The men gather their
   weapons.

23 OMITTED                23 *
```

```
                    13.

24 EXT. NIGHT SKY          24

   The moon is bright.

25 INT. GRANT'S TENT       25

   Soldiers enter and
   exit.  The general
   isn't here at the
   moment.  It's clear
   there's a great deal
   of tension in the air.
   CANNON FIRE can be
   heard IN the DISTANCE.

   Grant suddenly strides
   into the tent, jerks
   off his gloves and
   unrolls a map.  His
   face is covered with
   grime.
```

Material from the following pages can't be allowed to flow onto the revised page to fill the empty space, because if those pages have no changes, they aren't going to be reprinted. They must remain unchanged. This forces page 12 to remain a short page. It then fits correctly into the existing script.

"A" pages

But what do you do if enough new material is added to a page that it forces the subsequent text off the bottom of the page? Let's say that a couple of days have passed since the set of revisions described above. Today, a quarter-page scene needs to be added to page 13, but page 14 has no changes. The extra material from page 13 can't be allowed to flow onto page 14, because page 14 isn't going to be reprinted. Instead, page 13A is created to hold the overflow text and is printed along with the rest of the revised pages. Production personnel will pull the old page 13 out of their scripts and insert the new pages 13 and 13A in its place. The old page 14 will remain in the script unchanged and the new pages will fit correctly into the existing script:

```
         GRANT - Rev. 1/3/04 13.

24    EXT. NIGHT SKY          24

         The moon is bright.

24A  EXT. RIVER - NIGHT     24A*

         Confederate snipes        *
         wade silently across,     *
         their long, deadly        *
         rifles held high.         *

25    INT. GRANT'S TENT       25

         Soldiers enter and
         exit.  The general
         isn't here at the
         moment.  It's clear
         there's a great deal
         of tension in the air.

                     (CONTINUED)
```

```
         GRANT - Rev. 1/3/04 13A.

25    CONTINUED:              25

         CANNON FIRE can be
         heard IN the DISTANCE.

         Grant suddenly strides
         into the tent, jerks
         off his gloves and
         unrolls a map.  His
         face is covered with
         grime.
```

If needed, a "B" page can follow an "A" page, followed by a "C" page, and so on.

Runs of revised pages

When two or more pages in a row contain changes, they constitute a *run of revised pages*. Runs of pages receive special treatment. Since every page in the run has changes and is going to be reprinted, material can flow from page to page within the run. Say there are changes on pages 90, 91 and 92, but page 93 has no changes. A scene is deleted from page 90, making room for material from page 91 to flow forward onto page 90 and fill the empty space. Material from page 92 then flows forward onto page 91. Page 92, the last page in the run, becomes the short page. Page 93 remains undisturbed and the new pages fit correctly into the existing script:

123

```
        GRANT - Rev. 1/7/04 90.

51   EXT. WHITE HOUSE       51

     A military carriage
     rolls to a stop.
     General Grant and an
     aide step out.

52   OMITTED               52 *

53   INT. WHITE HOUSE       53
     CORRIDOR

     Grant and his aide are
     escorted inside.  The
     general is recognized.
     People stop to watch
     him pass.
```

```
        GRANT - Rev. 1/7/04 91.

54   INT. LINCOLN'S PRIVATE 54
     QUARTERS

     Grant and Lincoln
     confer in grave, soft
     voices.  Their words
     can't be made out.  The
     aide stands at a          *
     respectful distance.      *

     Finally Lincoln
     straightens and shakes
     the general's hand.


55   INT. WHITE HOUSE         55
     CORRIDOR

     Grant and his aide pass
     back out the way they     *
     came in.
```

```
        GRANT - Rev. 1/7/04 92.

56   EXT. VIRGINIA COUNTRY- 56
     SIDE - NIGHT

     Grant's special TRAIN
     CHUGS past in thick
     darkness, heading        *
     south.                   *
```

```
                             93.

57   EXT. DIRT ROAD - DAWN 57

     Grant rides astride a
     big gelding.  His
     aide trails him.
     They're riding fast,
     pushing their horses
     hard.


58   EXT. GRANT'S HEAD-       58
     QUARTERS - MORNING

     A hot sun is already
     shining.  A stir rises
     in the camp as Grant
     and his aide arrive.
     Grant dismounts and
     strides into his tent
     without a word to
     anyone.
```

Conversely, say that a scene is *added* to page 90. The extra material can flow onto pages 91 and 92 so long as they also have changes, and if an "A" page must be created it will come at the end of the run:

GRANT - Rev. 1/7/04 90.

51 EXT. WHITE HOUSE   51

    A military carriage
    rolls to a stop.
    General Grant and an
    aide step out.

51A WHITE HOUSE GUARDS   51A*

    Army troops guarding   *
    the executive residence *
    stand at attention.   *

52 ON GRANT   52

    He pauses to take in
    the great house that
    will one day be his.

                (CONTINUED)

GRANT - Rev. 1/7/04 91.

52 CONTINUED: 52

    His eyes travel up to
    a window in the
    private quarters. He
    sees the tall, stooped   *
    figure of the Pres-
    ident looking back at
    him.

53 INT. WHITE HOUSE   53
    CORRIDOR

    Grant and his aide are
    escorted inside. The
    general is recognized.
    People stop to watch
    him pass.

GRANT - Rev. 1/7/04 92.

54 INT. LINCOLN'S PRIVATE 54
    QUARTERS

    Grant and Lincoln
    confer in grave, soft
    voices. Their words
    can't be made out. The
    aide stands at a   *
    respectful distance.   *

    Finally Lincoln
    straightens and shakes
    the general's hand.

55 INT. WHITE HOUSE   55
    CORRIDOR

    Grant and his aide pass
    back out the way they   *
    came in.

                            93.

57 EXT. DIRT ROAD - DAWN 57

    Grant rides astride a
    big gelding. His
    aide trails him.
    They're riding fast,
    pushing their horses
    hard.

58 EXT. GRANT'S HEAD-   58
    QUARTERS - MORNING

    A hot sun is already
    shining. A stir rises
    in the camp as Grant
    and his aide arrive.
    Grant dismounts and
    strides into his tent
    without a word to
    anyone.

GRANT - Rev. 1/7/04 92A.

56 EXT. VIRGINIA COUNTRY- 56
    SIDE - NIGHT

    Grant's special TRAIN
    CHUGS past in thick
    darkness, heading   *
    south.   *

Managing page numbers when a script is revised

As material is added and deleted over time, "A" pages are created, other pages are deleted entirely, and numbering the pages properly becomes essential to helping everyone keep their scripts in the correct order with the current version of each page.

The basic numbering scheme for pages is the same as it is for scenes:

> Between 5 and 6 comes 5A.
> Between 5A and 6 comes 5B.
> Between 5A and 5B comes A5B.

The principle is that page A5 precedes page 5 and page 5A follows page 5.

If an entire page of text is deleted, it's essential to account for the page number so that everyone knows what has become of the page. If half of page 5 and all of page 6 are deleted (and page 7 has no changes), we end up with a page numbered 5/6. Production personnel will then understand that they throw away old pages 5 and 6 and replace them with the new page 5/6.

If multiple pages are deleted, the entire range of deleted page numbers must still be accounted for. To that end, we can issue a page numbered 14-18. Production personnel will discard all of the pages in that range and replace them with the new page 14-18.

Title pages distributed with revisions

When revised pages are distributed, they always include a title page printed on the new color of paper and listing the date and color of the revision:

Rev. 03/09/09 (Pink)

UNDER THE TABLE

written by
Jose Patrick Sladkey

FINAL DRAFT

March 7, 2009

As the above example shows, the date and draft of the last full script remain listed in the lower right corner of the title page and the date and color of the revised pages appear in the upper right corner of the page.

The dates and colors of subsequent sets of revised pages get added to the list at the top right of the title page as they are issued, with the date in six-digit format to keep things lined up:

```
Rev. 03/09/09 (Blue)
Rev. 03/13/09 (Pink)
Rev. 03/20/09 (Yellow)
Rev. 03/20/09 PM (Green)
Rev. 03/21/09 (Gold)
```

This list of revised dates and colors remains on the title page until a new full draft of the script is issued, if ever.

Note in the example above that a second set of revisions issued in the course of a single day bears the notation "PM" to distinguish it from the first set.

For more on title pages, see the section on *Special Pages*.

SPECIAL PAGES

Special script pages include *title pages*, *cast pages*, *sets pages*, *first pages, last pages* and pages containing *act breaks*.

Samples of many of these pages can be found in *Appendix C*.

Title pages

Every script needs a title page. The type of script will determine what information the title page should contain.

For a screenplay or teleplay written *on spec* (that is speculatively, not on assignment or under contract to a studio or producer), the title page should contain, at minimum, three pieces of information: 1) the title; 2) the name of the writer; and 3) contact information.

For a screenplay or teleplay written *under contract* to a studio or producer, the title page should contain 1) the title; 2) the name of the writer; 3) contact information, in this case the name of the studio or producer; and 4) the draft and date. It may also contain 5) a copyright notice.

1. *Title*

    The title is centered 4.0" below the top of the page, typed in all capital letters and underscored with one continuous underline. Quotation marks are not used.

    GONE WITH THE WIND

    For an episode of a television series, add the episode title, double-spaced beneath the series title, in upper and lower case letters, enclosed in quotation marks and underscored. The underline should not extend beneath the quotation marks.

    LAW AND ORDER

    "One for the Road"

2. *Name(s) and credit of the writer(s)*

    The writer's name and credit appear centered, beginning four lines below the title:

<u>12 HOURS IN BERLIN</u>

written by

Felix Alvin Butler Jr.

Name

The writer's name is typed in upper and lower case letters. If multiple writers are working as a team, their names are joined by an ampersand (&):

Felicia Keyes & Matthew Scott Brown

Credit

Screen credits in Hollywood are determined by the Writers Guild of America following shooting. Prior to that official determination, WGA rules require that the title page list the names of all writers who have worked on the project. The name of the first writer comes first, beneath the credit "written by," "screenplay by" or "teleplay by." The names of subsequent writers follow, beneath the credit "revisions by." The name of the current writer comes last, beneath the credit "current revisions by":

<u>12 HOURS IN BERLIN</u>

written by

Felix Alvin Butler Jr.

revisions by

Maria Gustav
Charles Knowles-Hilldebrand
Robert Bush

current revisions by

Johann Potemkin

3. ***Contact information***

For a spec script, you want the reader to know how to contact you if there's interest in your script. If you are not represented by an agent, manager or attorney, your address and/or phone number should appear in the lower left corner of the title page, beginning 1.2" from the left edge of the paper:

```
12902 Hollywood Place
Burbank, CA 91505
(818) 555-9807
```

For a script represented by an agent, manager or attorney, leave the writer's information off. The representative's contact information will appear on the title page, script cover or cover letter.

For a script written under contract, the studio or producer's contact information will appear:

```
MICHAEL GELD PRODUCTIONS
4000 Warner Boulevard
Burbank, CA 91505
```

4. ***Draft and date***

In order to help distinguish one version of a script from another, a script in development, preproduction or production ordinarily lists the script's draft and date in the lower right corner, beginning 5.5" in from the left edge of the paper. The draft is typed in all capital letters and underscored. The date is typed in upper and lower case letters, double-spaced beneath the draft:

FIRST DRAFT

March 3, 2009

A spec script has no real need to list a draft and date and can avoid appearing stale simply by leaving that information off the title page.

5. ***Copyright notice***

Some studios and production companies list a copyright notice on title pages of their scripts. This notice appears directly beneath the draft and date:

```
                                        REV. FINAL DRAFT

                                        May 2, 2009
                                        © 2009
                                        MICHAEL GELD PRODS.
                                        All Rights Reserved
```

Most spec scripts don't list a copyright notice or WGA registration number.

6.   ***When a script is based on other material or on a true story***

Information relating to source material for a script is listed beneath the writer's name, centered, in upper and lower case letters:

```
                    THE IMAGINARY WAR



                      screenplay by

                       Mari Zwick



                    based on the book by

                     Robert McMullen
```

Scripts based on, suggested by or inspired by true stories can indicate that fact in the same spot:

```
                   based on a true story
```

Cast pages

A cast page is usually included in an episodic television script at the preproduction stage. Some made-for-television movie scripts also incorporate cast pages. Feature film scripts and spec scripts do not.

A cast page follows the title page and lists the cast arranged either in order of appearance or according to some set order of regular cast, followed by the guest cast in order of appearance. The character names are typed in all capital letters at the left margin, beneath the title and the heading "CAST":

NINE LIVES

"Cats Away"

CAST

KITTY

JULIO MENDEZ

HILDE SCHMIDT

FELIX SIMPSON

LIEUTENANT MARTIN

For hour-long television and made-for-television movies, the list can wrap into a second column, if necessary.

Half-hour television scripts often include the names of the actors playing each role and a listing of any extras needed. The character name appears on the left side and the actor's name appears on the right. The names are connected by a dot leader:

NINE LIVES

"Cats Away"

CAST

KITTY...MARSHA WILLIAMS

JULIO MENDEZ...ALEX GONZALEZ

HILDE SCHMIDT.....................................ALISON PARMENTER

FELIX SIMPSON..............................MICHAEL PAUL MILLIKAN

LIEUTENANT MARTIN....................................ANTHONY BOGNA

PARKING LOT EXTRAS
POLICE HEADQUARTERS EXTRAS

Cast pages are not numbered.

135

Sets pages

A sets page, like a cast page, is usually included in an episodic television script at the preproduction stage. Some made-for-television movie scripts also incorporate sets pages. Feature film scripts and spec scripts do not.

For hour-long television and made-for-television movies, interior sets are listed in a column on the left side of the page and exterior sets are listed in a column on the right:

NINE LIVES

"Cats Away"

SETS

INTERIORS:	EXTERIORS:
KENNEDY HIGH SCHOOL	PARK
NEW YORK STOCK EXCHANGE	SCHOOL PLAYGROUND
STORM SEWERS	NEW YORK STOCK EXCHANGE
	DUMP

Sets are grouped logically. For example, if scenes take place in several different locations inside an elementary school, they get listed like this:

```
HAMMOND ELEMENTARY SCHOOL
     Library
     Cafeteria
     Mrs. Timberlake's
       Classroom
```

Sets pages are not numbered.

First pages

The first page of a script is unique in the following ways:

- Although it is counted as page 1, no page number is typed on the first page.

- The title is usually typed at the top of the first page, centered, in all capital letters and underscored. For episodic television, the episode title appears double-spaced beneath the series title, in upper and lower case letters, enclosed in quotation marks and underscored. The underline should not extend beneath the quotation marks.

- The first page virtually always begins with a FADE IN.

The first page of a script for a feature film or a made-for-television movie begins like this:

THE LONG SLIDE

FADE IN:

EXT. HIMALAYAS - HIGH ON WINDSWEPT PEAK

Snow and blinding sunshine.

The first page of an hour-long television episode begins like this:

NINE LIVES

"Cats Away"

ACT ONE

FADE IN:

EXT. PARK - DAY

KITTY sits high in the branches of a tree.

An example of the first page of a half-hour television script can be found in the section on *Multi-camera film format*.

Last pages

The last page of a script concludes with the words "THE END" typed in all capital letters, underscored and centered. If space allows, leave five blank lines between the final transition (e.g. FADE OUT or CUT TO BLACK) and "THE END." If space doesn't allow the full five blank lines, leave at least one blank line.

> Kitty climbs back into the tree and watches as the dilapidated school bus disappears into the night.
>
>   FADE OUT.
>
>
>
>   THE END

Act breaks

Scripts for episodic television shows and for many made-for-television movies contain act breaks, which represent the commercial breaks in the program. An hour-long television script usually consists of four acts. Half-hour scripts consist of either two or three acts. Two-hour movies typically consist of seven or eight acts. Some shows also include a teaser or prologue before the first act and/or an epilogue or tag after the last act.

A new act always begins at the top of a new page which includes a heading identifying the act in all capital letters, double-spaced beneath the page number, centered and underscored, followed by a transition double-spaced beneath it:

16.

ACT TWO

FADE IN:

INT. DETECTIVE BULLPEN - NIGHT

Savage slams a case file down on his desk. He picks up the
phone and punches in a number. He's not happy.

The last page of an act ends with a transition (usually FADE OUT) double-spaced below the
final script text, followed by the words "END OF ACT ONE" (or TWO or THREE, etc.) typed
in all capital letters, underscored and centered. If space allows, leave five blank lines between the
final transition (e.g. FADE OUT or CUT TO BLACK) and "END OF ACT ONE." If space
doesn't allow the full five blank lines, leave at least one blank line.

    Kitty races out the door in time to see McCloud wrestled
    aboard the bus. She pulls her gun and sprints for the BUS
    but it ROARS away, leaving her in a cloud of dust

                                        FADE OUT.

END OF ACT FIVE

The last page of the entire script ends with no reference to the number of the current act. Instead,
it ends with the words, "THE END." (See *Last pages* above.)

MULTI-CAMERA FORMAT

This is the format used for half-hour comedies shot in the classic sitcom style of *Two and a Half Men*, as opposed to the single-camera style of *The Office*. Much of what is true of single-camera film format and discussed in detail earlier in this guide is also true of multi-camera film format:

- The margins for shot headings, direction, dialogue and transitions are the same
- The same rules apply to font size and type, and paper size and type
- Shot headings are arranged according to the same rules
- The same rules apply to how dialogue and direction are broken between pages

The principle differences from single-camera film format are these:

- Shot headings and transitions are underscored
- Direction is typed in all capital letters
- Dialogue is double-spaced
- Sound cues are underscored
- Parenthetical character direction is embedded in dialogue

See *Appendix B* for sample script pages in multi-camera film format.

A million-dollar tip for anyone writing a spec television episode

Writers who aspire to write for television must write spec episodes of existing series to demonstrate their skill. To create the desired positive impression on agents and show runners, these spec episodes must be formatted like the scripts written by the show's staff writers. The challenge is that every television series, hour-long or half-hour, uses a slightly different format. The only sure way to know exactly what character names are used over dialogue, or what recurring locations are regularly called in shot headings, and countless other details that will help a spec script appear professional, is to obtain a copy of a sample episode. Study it. Replicate the format.

How to get your hands on a sample script?

In many cases, an Internet search will turn up an episode script online. Numerous sites host scripts, including:

- The Daily Script at http://www.dailyscript.com
- Drew's Script-O-Rama at http://www.script-o-rama.com
- The Internet Movie Script Database at http://imsdb.com
- Simply Scripts at http://www.simplyscripts.com
- Scriptcrawler at http://www.scriptcrawler.net

Pay attention to the type of script you're getting from these sites. Some are the actual scripts in their original formats. Others are transcripts created by fans, which won't be of any value to someone wanting to see how the show's actual scripts look. Jack Gilbert, an expert on television writing who has directed the vaunted Warner Bros. Writers Workshop, points out that scripts in PDF format are most likely to be copies of an original episode.

However, Gilbert recommends that the best source he's found for television scripts is http://tvwriting.googlepages.com. Next is Script City at www.scriptcity.net, which offers scripts in paper or PDF formats for about $10.

University libraries often contain sample scripts, especially if the school has a film and television writing program.

If you're in Southern California, visit the Writers Guild Foundation Shavelson-Webb Library to access their collection of upwards of 15,000 produced scripts. The library is housed in the WGA West headquarters at 7000 West Third Street, Los Angeles, CA 90048.

Standard multi-camera film format margins

Standard multi-camera film format margins are as follows:

1. **Paper** is 3-hole punched 8.5" x 11" white 20 lb. bond

2. **Shot headings**:
   Left margin is 1.7"
   Right margin is 1.1"
   Line length is 57 characters
   Shot headings are underscored

3. **Direction**:
   Left margin is 1.7"
   Right margin is 1.1"
   Line length is 57 characters
   Direction is typed in all capital letters

4. **Dialogue**:
   Left margin is 2.7"
   Right margin is 2.4"
   Line length is 34 characters
   Dialogue is typed in upper and lower case letters and double-spaced

5. **Character name over dialogue**:
   Left margin is 4.1"

   Note that the character name over dialogue is not centered. It begins at the same fixed point (4.1" from the left edge of the page) no matter how long it is

6.   **Parenthetical character direction** is embedded in dialogue in all capital letters

7.   **Scene transitions**:
> Left margin is 6.0"
> Scene transitions are underscored

8.   **Sound cues**:
> Left margin is 1.7"
> Right margin is 1.1"
> Line length is 57 characters
> Sound cues are typed in all capital letters and underscored and begin with the abbreviation SFX:

9.   **Scene letters**:
> Go at 7.2", on the line immediately following the page number
> Scene letters are capitalized and enclosed in parentheses

10.   **Page numbers**:
> Go at 7.2", .5" below the top edge of the paper

11.   **Font**:
> Courier or Courier New 12 point (or equivalent fixed-pitch serif font)

12.   **Page length**:
> A maximum of 57 lines (which allows for .5" margin at the top and 1" margin at the bottom of each page)
>
> These 57 lines include one line at the top of each page for the page number, followed by a blank line and the text of the script.

Shot Headings

Shot headings are arranged according to the principles detailed for single-camera film format.

The only change for multi-camera format is that shot headings are underscored:

```
INT. "BETTER FRED THAN DEAD" DINER - DAY
```

Typically multi-camera format scripts use very few shot headings besides master scene headings. It is common for a scene to run in its entirety beneath a single heading.

A new scene always begins on a new page. However, when action moves continuously from one room to an adjacent room and cameras don't stop rolling, a new shot heading may be used without it being considered a new scene. In this case, the new shot doesn't indicate a new scene but only a new portion of a continuing scene. Drop four lines after the final text of the first portion and type the new shot heading, like this:

<u>INT. DINER - KITCHEN - DAY</u>
(Fred)

FRED POURS PANCAKE BATTER ON THE GRIDDLE. TURNS ON THE DISHWATER. HE RUSHES OUT INTO:

<u>INT. MAIN DINER</u>

HE UNLOCKS THE FRONT DOOR. RUSHES BACK INTO:

<u>INT. KITCHEN</u>

HE FLIPS THE PANCAKES. THROWS DIRTY DISHES IN THE SINK.

Direction

Direction is typed in all capital letters. This of course alleviates the need to decide what to capitalize and greatly simplifies the task of formatting multi-camera format scripts:

IT'S THE BREAKFAST RUSH. FRED'S BEHIND THE COUNTER. MARTHA'S TAKING AN ORDER FROM DEBBIE, EARLY 20S, ATHLETIC, LEAN.

Underscoring character entrances and exits

Character entrances and exits are underscored in direction. Underscore the name of the character and the word or words describing the entrance or exit:

THE DOOR OPENS. <u>BOB ENTERS</u>.

<u>CURT COMES THROUGH THE FRONT DOOR</u> AND SLIPS ON A BANANA PEEL.

<u>BEICHMAN</u> GRABS A BUCKET AND <u>EXITS</u> AT A RUN.

Underscoring camera direction

Camera direction is underscored in direction. Underscore the word camera as well as any words related to the camera's movement and associated prepositions:

```
SWEETPEA SITS ALONE ON A CHAIR, READING THE LETTER.  HER
BODY IS RACKED WITH SILENT SOBS.  CAMERA PULLS BACK TO
REVEAL THAT THE ENTIRE ACTING CLASS SURROUNDS HER, WIPING
AWAY TEARS AT HER BRAVURA PERFORMANCE.
```

Dialogue

Character names over dialogue follow the same rules as those for single-camera film format. The dialogue itself is typed in upper and lower-case letters and double-spaced:

                         FRED

          That's it! First Johnny called and

          said he had the flu. Now Ronnie

          calls with a cold. The job is a

          real headache.

                         MARTHA

          I've gotta tell you. All this

          moaning and groaning is making me

          sick!

Using (CONT'D) when dialogue continues after an interruption

Whenever the same character continues speaking after an interruption for direction or a sound cue, the abbreviation (CONT'D) is placed beside the character's name over dialogue, typed in all capital letters, inside parentheses:

                         DEBBIE

            Ronnie, come over here.

      RONNIE APPROACHES, FILLED WITH TREPIDATION.

> DEBBIE (CONT'D)
>
> Come closer. I'm not gonna hurt
>
> you.

Parenthetical character direction

All the rules from single-camera film format apply here, with one important exception. In multi-camera format, parenthetical character direction is embedded in the dialogue, not pulled out on a separate line at a separate tab:

> FRED
>
> Eyes this way, people. (WAITS)
>
> So that's about it. (TURNS TO
>
> O.S. AUDIENCE) How'd we do?

Transitions

Scene transitions follow the same rules in multi-camera format that they do in single-camera film format. The only difference here is that they get underscored:

> CUT TO:
>
> WIPE TO:
>
> DISSOLVE TO:
>
> FADE OUT.
>
> RIPPLE DISSOLVE TO:

Sound cues

All *sound cues* (sounds that must be made by someone besides an actor on camera) are underscored and preceded by the abbreviation "SFX":

> CURT HITS THE FLOOR. MOANS LIKE A COW.
>
> SFX: THE PHONE RINGS.

```
NO ON ANSWERS IT.  CURT LOOKS UP FROM WHERE HE LIES ON THE
FLOOR.
```

Character listings

Characters who appear in a scene are listed beneath the shot heading for that scene. They are typed in the order of appearance, in upper and lower case letters, inside parentheses, with extras listed after speaking characters:

```
INT. "BETTER FRED THAN DEAD" DINER - DAY
(Fred, Martha, Bob, Debbie, Curt, Diner Extras)

IT'S THE BREAKFAST RUSH.  FRED'S BEHIND THE COUNTER.
MARTHA'S TAKING AN ORDER FROM DEBBIE.
```

Scene numbers or letters

Scenes in a multi-camera script are either lettered or numbered. Most often they are lettered. The scene letter appears capitalized, inside parentheses, on each page of the scene.

First page of a scene

Practices vary from series to series, but the following is a common and time-honored scheme. On the first page of a scene, the scene letter is centered, 12 lines below the top of the page. The text of the scene begins 12 lines below that:

21.

(D)

INT. FRED'S APARTMENT - NIGHT
(Fred, Martha)

FRED ENTERS TO FIND MARTHA TRYING TO WRESTLE THE
REFRIGERATOR OUT AN OPEN WINDOW.

Subsequent pages

All subsequent pages that are part of the scene show the scene letter directly below the page
number. The text of the script begins on the line immediately below the scene letter:

45.
(G)

CURT PLACES THE CHAIRS ON TOP OF THE TABLES.

First pages of acts

Like hour-long television and many made-for-television movies, half-hour television scripts are
divided into acts. Some also include a teaser, cold open, or prologue and a tag or epilogue.

Page one

The first page of a multi-camera script includes the series and episode titles plus the heading ACT ONE, TEASER or PROLOGUE, as appropriate, typed in all capitals letters, underscored and centered:

BETTER FRED THAN DEAD

"A Simple Sample"

ACT ONE

(A)

FADE IN:

INT. "BETTER FRED THAN DEAD DINER - DAY
(Fred, Martha, Debbie, Bob, Curt, Diner Extras)

IT'S THE BREAKFAST RUSH. FRED'S BEHIND THE COUNER.
MARTHA'S TAKING AN ORDER FROM DEBBIE.

The scene letter appears on line 12 and the text of the script begins on line 24. As with single-camera film format, the page number is not typed on page 1.

First pages of subsequent acts

The first page of each subsequent act begins with the act heading (e.g. ACT TWO) typed in capital letters, centered and underscored on line 3, followed by the scene letter on line 12 and the text of the script beginning on line 24:

30.

<u>ACT THREE</u>

(G)

<u>FADE IN:</u>

<u>INT. CURT'S TAXI - NIGHT</u>
(Curt, Customer Extra)

CURT DRIVES. HE'S WHISTLING A TUNE. AT FIRST IT'S HARD TO
MAKE OUT WHAT IT IS.

Last page of each act

The last page of an act ends with a transition (usually FADE OUT) double-spaced below the
final script text, followed by the words "END OF ACT ONE" (or TWO or THREE, etc.) typed
in all capital letters, underscored and centered. If space allows, leave five blank lines between the
final transition (e.g. FADE OUT or CUT TO BLACK) and "END OF ACT ONE." If space
doesn't allow the full five blank lines, leave at least one blank line.

FRED CLOSES THE DOOR TO THE DINER AND SHUTS OFF THE LIGHTS.

<u>FADE OUT.</u>

<u>END OF ACT ONE</u>

The last page of the entire script ends with no reference to the number of the current act. Instead, it ends with the words, "THE END."

Breaking pages

The following rules govern the breaking of pages in multi-camera film format scripts.

No CONTINUEDs

When a scene continues from one page to the next, no (CONTINUED) is placed at the bottom of one page and no CONTINUED: appears at the top of the next. The scene simply continues.

Breaking dialogue

When a speech is broken at the bottom of a page, always break at the end of a sentence and add (MORE) at the bottom of the first page, double-spaced beneath the dialogue, and (CONT'D) at the top of the following page beside the character name:

```
                    CURT

      This is the last time I come in

      here expecting to be served

      something that's actually, how

      do you say, edible.

                    (MORE)
```

```
                                        12.
                                        (B)

                  CURT (CONT'D)

      Can I just have a bottle of water

      and some crackers?
```

Even when direction interrupts the speech, (MORE) and (CONT'D) are still required:

```
                      FRED

          Comin' atcha.

    HE CLIMBS ONTO THE DINER COUNTER.

                    (MORE)
```

```
                                                  7.
                                                  (A)

                  FRED (CONT'D)

          Yo.  Yo yo.  Your attention right

          here, if you please.
```

Note that (MORE) is typed beneath the interrupting line of direction, as the last word on the page.

Breaking direction

When breaking direction from one page to the next, always break at the end of a sentence:

```
    CURT CLIMBS TO HIS FEET.   FRED CLAPS HIS HANDS FOR
    ATTENTION.
```

```
                                                  24.
                                                  (E)

    EVERYONE IN THE DINER STANDS, FACES CURT AND APPLAUDS.
```

Breaking near a sound cue

When breaking a page near a sound cue, arrange the break so that the sound cue is not the first item at the top of a page. If a sound cue won't fit at the bottom of a page, carry it to the top of the next page along with the dialogue or direction that immediately precedes it:

```
    CURT COMES THROUGH THE FRONT DOOR AND SLIPS ON THE BANANA
    PEEL.   HE TAKES OUT AN ENTIRE ROW OF TABLES ON HIS WAY
    DOWN.   IT'S A SIGHT TO BEHOLD.
```

3.
(A)

DEBBIE

I stand corrected.

SFX: THE PHONE RINGS.

NO ONE ANSWERS IT. CURT LOOKS UP FROM WHERE HE LIES ON THE
FLOOR.

Breaking near a shot heading

A shot heading can't appear as the last item at the bottom of a page. At least one full sentence of direction must accompany the shot heading or it should be moved to the top of the next page.

Breaking before a scene transition

Never break a page immediately before a transition. If a transition won't fit at the bottom of a page, carry it to the top of the next page along with the dialogue or direction that immediately precedes it:

4.
(A)

EVERYONE IN THE DINER STANDS, FACES THE AUDIENCE AND
BOWS.

DISSOLVE TO:

UNLEASHING THE POWER OF SCRIPT TYPING SOFTWARE

Photographers need cameras. Painters need brushes. And screenwriters need computers. We used to need typewriters, but that was a long time ago. Now we need computers. *Need* them. And why is that exactly? What do computers do for us that typewriters never could?

As we begin a discussion about computer hardware and software, it's useful to review the job this technology should be doing for us as it relates to putting our scripts on the page.

Back in the day...

In the beginning there were Underwoods. Big, noisy monstrosities that had the remarkable ability to put words on paper in whatever order and configuration the writer wished, including standard screenplay format. No batteries ever ran low. There was no toner to buy, no drum unit, no ink cartridge, no software upgrade. The keyboard and printer were built into the device and the thing was virtually incapable of jamming or breaking down. Once in a while a ribbon needed to be replaced. Other than that, the Underwood just spit out script pages.

Unfortunately, if you wanted to add a line, delete a word or flip-flop the order of two paragraphs, you had to retype the whole page. Often you had to retype the whole dang script. Either that or cut and paste with literal scissors and cellophane tape. And you had to find your own typos by actually reading the page you'd written. And correcting the typos you found was no picnic. And if your finished screenplay fell off the copy boy's bicycle on the way to the mimeo department and blew away, well, it was simply gone. The only backup copy was locked somewhere in your imperfect memory.

Flash forward to the wireless future

Today, of course, everything has changed. The Underwood is a relic and the wireless home network is everywhere. Let's review what the new electronics have brought to our big Hollywood party:

- Computers let us make changes to an existing script page with ease, which means we no longer have to weigh the physical difficulty of making a script change. We just do it.

- Computers loaded with script typing software provide automatic margin changes as we move effortlessly from dialogue to direction to shot headings and back again.

- Computers allow us to spell-check our work and can give us access to an electronic dictionary and thesaurus and even screenwriting advice.

- Computers provide crisp, flawless original printouts of script pages, free from White-Out smudges and erasure holes.

- Computers can print as many of those flawless originals as we like.

- Computers provide numerous ways for us to back up our work and protect it from rain, flood, fire — and a few viruses the Underwood never seemed to catch.

- Computers even allow us to transmit our scripts electronically and virtually instantaneously anywhere in the world, opening up unimagined doors of possibility for collaboration.

There's no question we're immensely better off with computers. The challenge is making sure we reap the maximum benefit from the technology without surrendering control of the final product to a piece of computer equipment or programming. We mustn't trade that ability to create script pages that are correctly and professionally formatted for pages that are simply easy to produce. Which brings us to the next part of our discussion.

What computers can't do

A computer can't write your movie for you. Obviously. No more than the paintbrush can create a masterpiece without the artist. But here's what we sometimes miss. A computer can't *format* your script for you, either.

Surprised?

Look back at the list above. Yes, computers armed with good software will apply standard margins to a shot heading or a scene transition. But the software can't tell you where to put the shot heading, what information to include, what to leave out. It can't help you with sound or camera capping in direction. It can't tell you where to paragraph or what belongs in parenthetical character direction or whether you ought to underscore or capitalize or italicize words in dialogue for emphasis. It won't tell you that your establishing shot isn't really an establishing shot, or that you need to yank Huck out of Huck's POV. All of that has to come from you. From your knowledge of standard Hollywood script format. Computer software, by itself, will never be enough. Don't ask it to do a job it was never designed to do.

Choosing the right software

So which program should you use? It depends on who you are and what you want the software to do.

The first rule of choosing computer software to use in writing scripts is simply this: **Choose the program that best helps you put your script on the page.** That's its job. To help you, the writer, put the words where you want them, not where the software wants them. If a program is

155

preventing you from laying out your script the way you see fit, if it's dictating to you and inhibiting your control over your own work, then it's the wrong program.

Second, **choose the program that provides the features you need**. Are you going to be writing spec scripts only? Then you don't necessarily need software that meets the rigorous demands of production. Are you working with a writing partner? Choose a program that's compatible with your partner's. Are you typing scripts for a television series in production? You need software that allows you to control the numbering of scenes and pages, the placement of revision marks and the content of the revision slug.

Finally, **choose the program that fits your budget.** One popular program retails for over $200. Another is free. While these programs aren't identical in their features, you don't have to wait until you've saved $200 to get started writing.

You have several approaches to choose from.

Do-it-yourself software solutions

Many writers work within a robust word processing software like Microsoft Word or WordPerfect, using a personalized set of macros and styles to apply margins to their scripts. Warner Bros. for many years used a complex set of macros in conjunction with WordPerfect for typing scripts. This approach allows a computer-savvy writer maximum control over the various elements of a script but provides less automation than commercial script software.

Commercial script software

Many other writers swear by one of several commercial script typing programs on the market ranging in price from about $50 to $250. Some are complete, stand-alone programs:

•   Final Draft

•   Movie Magic Screenwriter

•   Scriptware

•   Page 2 Stage

Others work within Microsoft Word:

•   HollyWord

•   Script Wright

•   ScriptWerx

•   Script Wizard

And at least one is available as a free download:

- Celtx

Each of these programs automates various parts of the script typing process. The features of various programs are constantly evolving, but usually include many of the following:

- Preset margins for screenplays (what I call in this manual "single-camera film format"), sitcoms ("multi-camera film format") and stage plays

- Import/export of files to and from various common file formats, including Rich Text Format, Adobe Acrobat's PDF and HTML

- Automatic typing of repeated character names and master shot headings (e.g. you type CAPT and the software completes CAPTAIN VON TRAPP)

- Spell check

- Thesaurus

- Index card systems that allow for the simplified reshuffling of scenes

- Online writing advice about such things as plot, structure and character

- Automatic revision marks

- A and B scene and page numbers

- Colored pages for revisions

Of the commercial script typing programs currently on the market, Final Draft is the best-selling. That carries certain benefits, among them file compatibility with large numbers of other writers and producers. But you should choose the program with the features that are important to the way you are going to work. And don't settle for software that doesn't allow you to put the words where you know they belong.

Don't let the autopilot fly you into the ground

Many writers get lulled into believing that their scripts are professionally formatted simply because they're typed using a best-selling script program. They're wrong. As helpful as these programs are, the writer is still the writer. If the software wants to add "(continuing)" every time a character's dialogue is interrupted by direction, don't let it if that's not what you want. If the software's autotype feature wants to repeat precisely the same master scene heading every time you return to a location, don't let it. You're the writer. You know better. You decide what goes in the shot heading. Don't let the computer make creative decisions for you. That isn't its job. It's yours. You're the writer. You know better.

Mac vs. PC

As fraught with emotion as this question sometimes becomes, this is an easy one. Writers use both Macintosh and IBM-PC based computers. Both work. Choose a computer that runs the software you want to use and is compatible with anyone with whom you expect to collaborate.

Printers

If there are still any dot-matrix printers out there, put them out of their misery. Laser-quality printing is standard in Hollywood. That means a true laser printer (Brother sells one for less than $100) or a good inkjet printer capable of at least 600 dpi (available from Epson and Canon, among others, for well under $100). Never send out a page that doesn't look perfect.

Backup

One of the great benefits of typing scripts on a computer is that you can easily save copies of every draft and keep multiple backups in multiple locations to prevent against the catastrophic loss of your work due to fire or some other disaster. Don't neglect to back up your work. You're investing countless hours of creativity in a script that, if not properly safeguarded, can disappear at the speed of light.

While you're writing

Make sure the autosave feature is enabled and is frequently backing up your work as you go, at least once every ten minutes. The worst that can happen, in the event of a power failure or computer crash, is that you'll lose ten minutes' worth of work.

When you quit for the day

Before you walk away from your computer, back up your work to a removable medium, a flash drive, a CD, a tape drive or even a paper printout — something that will survive if your hard drive doesn't. This ensures that the worst that can happen, even if the hard drive dies in the middle of the day, is that you'll lose only one day's work.

At least once a week

Store a backup copy of your script at a remote location. That can mean a paper copy, flash drive or CD kept in the car or office, or a copy of the file stored in free online storage such as that provided by Yahoo. Another solution is simply to email the file to yourself, with an account like

Gmail that stores your messages online. That way, even if your computer and CDs melt in a fire or get crushed by stampeding bison, your script will endure.

File-naming protocol

If you're working as hard as you should be, you'll produce numerous drafts of each project you write. The best way to keep all those files straight is to use a set file-naming protocol. Here's mine.

First I give the project a short name. Let's say my movie is called PEARL HARBOR SAVED MY LIFE. For purposes of backup, I'll call the project PEARL. The very first version of the project will get saved as PEARL01, with whatever file extension is appropriate, such as .doc or .fdr. The next version will be PEARL02. Then comes PEARL03. That's all there is to it. It's simple, it's easy, the file names stay short and I never have to guess which version came when.

When to change the file version number

How often should you give the file a new name by increasing the version number, changing PEARL05 to PEARL06? As often as necessary to maintain a record of what you've written. Let's say you start PEARL05 as a page-one rewrite. On the first day you write pages 1 through 4. The next day you keep going and write pages 5 through 8. No need to rename the file. You're only building on the existing draft. Just keep saving the growing file under the name PEARL05. But then one day after you reach page 60, you decide to go back and revise the first half of your movie. Now you want to increase the version number so that you keep a record of those first 60 pages. Rename the file PEARL06 before you make your changes. If you ever want to go back and look at something from PEARL05, you'll have it.

SEARCH AND DESTROY: THE SCOURGE OF TYPOS AND THE POWER OF PROOFREADING

Don't squander everything you've learned about professional script format and the intense creative effort you've made writing your script by failing to proofread your work before showing it to readers. A classic line like "To be or not to be" loses a good deal of its punch when it's typed "Too be ore knot t6 bee."

The Zen of proofreading

Proofreading differs dramatically from ordinary reading. When we read, we swallow words whole. Our eye skips across the surface of sentences, constructing meaning at lightning speed, without laboring over every individual character. It's how we read as quickly as we do. It's also why we miss so many of our own typos. We see what we expect to see. We see what ought to be there. But when we proofread, we must force ourselves to read every letter, every scrap of punctuation, the characters that are actually there, not the ones we meant to put there.

This requires a whole new skill. And a good deal of effort. We have to slow ourselves down. Discipline our eye. See the page.

But that's only part of it.

We have to know what we're looking for.

What we're looking for

We're looking for misspellings. They're easy to spot while the script is still on the computer screen, underlined in wavy red lines. Search for them and correct them.

We're looking for the wrong words, correctly spelled. "Choose" when we mean "chose." "Conscious" when we mean "conscience." "Lay" when we mean "lie." "Now" when we mean "not." Or "General Motors" when we mean "Major Payne." The wavy red lines don't help us here. Only a careful, disciplined, slow reading of our pages will root out these errors.

We're looking for more of the wrong words, correctly spelled. Homophones. Those pesky sound-alike words we regularly mistake for one another:

- whose vs. who's
- to vs. too vs. two
- affect vs. effect

- lead vs. led
- its vs. it's
- brake vs. break
- pedal vs. petal vs. peddle
- illusion vs. allusion
- then vs. than

We're looking for punctuation errors. Periods missing at the ends of sentences. Question marks missing at the ends of questions. Commas missing in direct address.

We're looking for capitalization errors. Proper names missing a capital letter. Capital letters where they don't belong. Offscreen sounds, camera direction and character introductions you've failed to capitalize.

We're looking for omissions. A speech that has inexplicably vanished. A dropped word. A scene gone AWOL.

We're looking for dialogue formatted as direction, or direction formatted as dialogue. Character names missing over dialogue. Shot headings masquerading as scene transitions.

Three steps to clean copy

Tackle proofreading in three distinct steps. Three search-and-destroy missions through the pages of your script.

Step one. Scroll slowly through your entire script on the screen. Find every case where the electronic spell-checker indicates a misspelling and either correct it or overrule your spell-checker.

Step two. Print a hard copy of your script and read slowly through every character, every punctuation mark, every word. Set aside at least two minutes per page for this step. If you can do it much faster than this, you're missing things. With a red pen, mark every correction you find. Beside every correction, make a big X or checkmark in the margin so you don't miss it when you return to make the changes.

Step three. Comb through your script page by page, making each correction on the screen that you've made on the page. Here's where your red pen and checkmarks in the margin help you. Make the changes carefully so you don't introduce new errors into the text.

A fourth step for economy

Read your script again. This time, you're looking for words to cut. Examine every shot heading and ask whether it can be streamlined by omitting a word or two or three. In every sentence of direction, search out words that don't pull their weight. Eliminate them. Don't repeat in direction what you've just stated in a shot heading. In dialogue, less is more. Characters shouldn't tell us what we already know, especially if we've just seen it. Cut, cut, cut. The quality of the read can improve dramatically simply through the trimming of verbal fat.

Because we're human, a fifth step

Find someone else to proofread your script and find the errors you've overlooked. Recruit a grammar nerd. Someone who knows his dangling participles and split infinitives. Someone who isn't you. Loan him your red pen. You'll be mortified to see how much you've missed. And relieved to have caught all those mistakes before you send your script to CAA.

Please, please, please don't ask a busy agent, executive, producer or reader to read your script until you have.

On behalf of everyone who reads scripts for a living, thank you.

A FINAL WORD

Screenplays and teleplays are more than technical documents. They are a form of literature in their own right, separate from the films and television programs that may be made from them. And just as the layout of a poem on the page is an integral part of the poetry, so is format an integral part of the art of the script.

Use the guidelines in this manual as a launching point for your creativity. Properly understood, they should never hold you back. Instead, use the principles contained in this book as tools *to free you* to express clearly and powerfully your artistic vision, to capture on the script page the best and deepest and truest things you know.

Write with all your heart. Advance the art of the screenplay.

APPENDIX A

Single-camera film format

Sample Script Pages

PERFECT PITCH

FADE IN:

EXT. VAN NUYS APARTMENT - MORNING

A 12-year-old tagger, not unlike a pit bull, leaves his mark on a fire hydrant outside this dreary stucco complex.

It's a picture-perfect day in the Valley. Not a cloud in the beige sky.

An ALARM CLOCK GOES OFF.

INT. STUDIO APARTMENT

A feminine arm shoots out of the covers and gropes a bedside table for the ALARM. Knocks a pair of glasses onto the floor. Keeps searching. Tips an empty coffee mug onto its side. Finally finds the clock and hits snooze. The ALARM GOES SILENT.

The arm drops back onto the bed.

The ALARM CLOCK TICKS.

VENETIAN BLINDS

RATTLE almost imperceptibly.

OVERTURNED COFFEE MUG

rocks gently back and forth.

WIDE ON APARTMENT

Silence for the longest time. Then all hell breaks loose.

The ROOM SHAKES VIOLENTLY. The bed hops like a spastic rabbit. Pictures drop off the walls.

The COFFEE MUG falls and SHATTERS.

ASPIRING SCREENWRITER

explodes from beneath the covers, eyes wide with terror as her APARTMENT QUAKES around her. GRETCHEN PFLUM.

166

Beside her bed a computer monitor sways violently, tips and topples.

Gretchen dives. Gets tangled in the sheets. Hits the floor just as the MONITOR SMASHES over the top of the printer.

And then it ALL STOPS. Just like that. Gretchen looks around the apartment. It's an unbelievable mess. So's she. Early 20s, she's rumpled and badly shaken. But so darn cute you don't care.

Seven seconds of silence. And then the PIPES over her head BURST. WATER DRENCHES the apartment.

EXT. GRETCHEN'S APARTMENT - MORNING

The door is flung open. Gretchen staggers outside. Rumpled, shaken and now soaked. But still cute. CAR ALARMS are BLARING. DOGS are BARKING. Neighbors are spilling from their apartments. Gretchen looks around, spots an elderly woman in a muumuu.

                     GRETCHEN
          Stella, what just happened? What
          was that?!

STELLA toddles toward Gretchen, utterly unruffled.

                     STELLA
          Oh, I'd say about a six point one
          or six point two. Have a muffin,
          dear.
                    (hands Gretchen one
                     and glances at her
                     watch)
          Didn't you have a meeting this
          morning?

Gretchen blanches.

                     GRETCHEN
          Oh no.

INT. GRETCHEN'S APARTMENT

She appears in the doorway. WATER continues to RAIN DOWN.

                     GRETCHEN
          Oh no.

She plunges into the room.

Steps over fallen items to her computer. Sees the
shattered monitor atop the printer.

                    GRETCHEN
          OH NO.
                    (a cry from the
                    depths)
          MY PITCH!!!!!!!!!!

She starts to dig. Heaves the monitor to the floor. Her
PHONE RINGS. She looks for it. Can't find it. It KEEPS
RINGING. In frustration she kicks the monitor shell.
Unearthing the phone. She answers.

                    GRETCHEN
          Hello?

                    GRETCHEN'S MAMA (V.O.)
          Baby?

INTERCUT WITH:

EXT. KANSAS FARM - ENDLESS WHEAT FIELD - DAY

GRETCHEN'S MAMA in the air-conditioned, glassed-in
cockpit of a massive, modern combine, mowing down wheat.
She's got a cell phone to her ear. A RADIO PLAYS LOW in
the b.g.

                    GRETCHEN
          Mama?

                    GRETCHEN'S MAMA
          Listen, baby, I can't talk long
          but I want you to Fed Ex me some
          more of that good mango salsa.

Gretchen picks gingerly through the broken glass that
litters her computer equipment. She pulls a stack of
soggy pages from the printer.

                    GRETCHEN'S MAMA
          Your father and I drizzled it over
          our grilled salmon last night
          and --

                    GRETCHEN
                    (starting to cry)
          Mama, I just had an earthquake.

                    GRETCHEN'S MAMA
          An earthquake? Are you sure,
          baby?

                    GRETCHEN
                 (crying harder)
          Of course I'm sure --

                  GRETCHEN'S MAMA
          Because I've got on C.N.N. and
          they're not saying a thing about
          an earthquake.

Gretchen looks at the destruction all around her.
Doesn't know what to say.

                    GRETCHEN
          Mama, I've got to go. I have a
          very important meeting and I
          overslept and then the earthquake
          woke me up --

                  GRETCHEN'S MAMA
          Well there you go! Blessing in
          disguise.
                    (then)
          Gotta go, baby. Don't forget the
          salsa. Kisses.

She clicks off. Leaving Gretchen remembering why she
fled Kansas in the first place.

                                      CUT TO:

EXT. APARTMENT BUILDING - PARKING LOT - GRETCHEN'S CAR -
DAY

A WHIMPERING sound as Gretchen rushes up, dressed, her
hair still wet. She hears the sound and looks around.
Sees nothing. Unlocks her door. The WHIMPERING again.
She looks beneath her car.

HER POV UNDER CAR

A dirty, frightened CHIHUAHUA cowers, CRYING.

                    GRETCHEN (O.S.)
          Hey there, Taco Bell, what's
          wrong?

BACK TO SCENE

Gretchen extends her arms. The dog races from under her
car and leaps into them. She laughs.

                    GRETCHEN
          Earthquake scare you, little guy?
                    (beat)
          Listen, I've got to run. Where do
          you belong?

The little dog licks her face.

EXT. STUDIO GATE - DAY

Gretchen pulls up to the guard shack in her '83 Civic. A
GUARD steps up to the car.

                    GUARD
          Going to see?

                    GRETCHEN
                    (intimidated)
          Ian von Blitzenkrantz.

                    GUARD
          The producer?
                    (looks over her sad
                    little car)
          Here to dust his Oscars?

Something rises up inside Gretchen. She is, after all, a
screenwriter.

                    GRETCHEN
          No, I'm not here to dust his
          Oscars. I'm here to win him
          another one.

The Guard is duly impressed by her moxy.

                    GUARD
          Name?

                    GRETCHEN
          Gretchen Pflum. P-F-L-U-M.

The Guard checks his list.

                    GUARD
          Don't see it.
                    (looks inside car)
          And you can't bring in the dog.

The little chihuahua sits on the passenger seat. Eating
Gretchen's pitch.

                    GRETCHEN
          No, no, no!!!

She pulls the half-eaten pages from the dog's mouth.
They're beyond salvage.

                    GRETCHEN
          Oh noooooooooo!!!

INT. PRODUCER'S OFFICES - RECEPTION AREA - DAY

A hard-driving young executive WANNA-BE jabbers into a
telephone headset while he surfs the Web. Everything he
says he says fast.

                    WANNA-BE
          Von Blitzenkrantz Entertainment...
          He'sinameetingcanwereturn?

He looks up as Gretchen enters.

                    WANNA-BE
               (to phone)
          Holdplease.
               (to Gretchen)
          Helpyou?

                    GRETCHEN
          Gretchen Pflum. I have a meeting
          with Mr. von Blitzenkrantz. I
          may be a little, um... late.

                    WANNA-BE
          HaveaseatI'lllethimknowyou'rehere.
          Wantanythingtodrink?
          Coffeesodawater?

Gretchen takes a beat to decode his spiel.

                    GRETCHEN
          Oh. Well. Um. Water.

She smiles.

                    WANNA-BE
          Bottled or tap?

                    GRETCHEN
          Oh. Um. Bottled.

                    WANNA-BE
          Perrier or Evian?

                    GRETCHEN
          ... Perrier.

                         WANNA-BE
              Room temperature or refrigerated?

Gretchen just stares.

                                        DISSOLVE TO:

INT. RECEPTION AREA - LATER

Time has passed. Lots of time. The bottle of Perrier is
empty. Gretchen's trying to piece together what's left
of her tattered pitch. The Wanna-Be is still on the
phone.

                         WANNA-BE
              NoIhaven'treadthescriptI'vereadthe
              coverage. Greatcoverage. Huge
              coverage. BestcoverageI'veever
              read. PluginOrlandoorMattorWill
              andyou'vegotahit.

                                        DISSOLVE TO:

INT. RECEPTION AREA - LATER

The Wanna-Be is gone. Gretchen still waits. Finally, a
voice like a foghorn bellows from O.S.

                         VOICE (O.S.)
              Jason?!... Jason?!... Jason?!...
              Jason?!

A puffy-faced guy in his 50s pads out in his bare feet.
IAN VON BLITZENKRANTZ. He sees there's no one behind the
desk. Spots Gretchen.

                         VON BLITZENKRANTZ
              Who are you?

                         GRETCHEN
              Gretchen Pflum. I'm supposed to
              pitch to Mr. von Blitzenkrantz.

He stares at her an uncomfortably long moment. At long,
long last:

                         VON BLITZENKRANTZ
              Okey-dokey.

INT. VON BLITZENKRANTZ'S OFFICE - DAY

Movie posters from his Oscar-winning films cover the
walls. Statuettes litter the desk. Gretchen sits on the
couch, dry-mouthed and tongue-tied, leafing through the
pages of her prepared pitch. Von Blitzenkrantz waits.

                    VON BLITZENKRANTZ
          So, sweetheart. Now's when you
          tell me a story.

Gretchen looks up like a deer caught in the headlights.
Clears her throat. Sets the pages aside. And begins.

                    GRETCHEN
          A studio apartment in Van Nuys.
          An alarm clock is ringing.
          There's a girl --

                    VON BLITZENKRANTZ
          How old?

                    GRETCHEN
          Early twenties.

                    VON BLITZENKRANTZ
          Good. We'll get that chick from
          "Alias."

                    GRETCHEN
          The girl's in bed. She's
          overslept.

                    VON BLITZENKRANTZ
          Who's she with?

                    GRETCHEN
          Who's she with? Um... she's
          alone.

                    VON BLITZENKRANTZ
          She's alone?
               (guffaws)
          How interesting is that?!
               (then)
          No, seriously.

                    GRETCHEN
          Well... okay... she's not
          completely alone. There's a dog.

                    VON BLITZENKRANTZ
          What kind of dog?

                    GRETCHEN
Chihuahua.

                    VON BLITZENKRANTZ
Chihuahuas are hot right now. I
like the way you think.

                    GRETCHEN
Then this massive earthquake hits.
<u>BANG</u>!!!

She slams her hand down on the coffee table. Von
Blitzenkrantz nearly jumps out of his skin. He cocks his
head and studies Gretchen. At long last throws his hands
straight up in the air and exclaims:

                    VON BLITZENKRANTZ
<u>I love this stuff</u>!!!
                    (stands)
I gotta pee.
                    (heads for the door)
But you keep going. You're doing
great.

He disappears. Gretchen looks around the empty office.
Shrugs. And keeps going.

                    GRETCHEN
So the bed starts jumping around
like a spastic rabbit, the girl is
like insane with fear --

Gretchen gets up and crosses to the enormous desk.
Admires the Oscars there.

                    GRETCHEN
But she doesn't care, she's got
the first pitch meeting of her
life and nothing is going to stop
her.

She spots a little dust on one of the statuettes. Buffs
it with her sleeve.

                    GRETCHEN
But then she sees her computer
monitor about to crash onto her
only copy of her perfect,
wonderful pitch. She dives! <u>And</u>
<u>snatches that bad boy out of the</u>
<u>air</u>!!!

Gretchen smiles like the sunrise.   'Cause she's in
Hollywood now.

                                        FADE OUT.

                          THE END

APPENDIX B

Multi-camera film format

Sample Script Pages

BETTER FRED THAN DEAD

"A Simple Sample"

ACT ONE

(A)

FADE IN:

INT. "BETTER FRED THAN DEAD" DINER - DAY
(Fred, Martha, Debbie, Bob, Curt, Diner Extras)

IT'S THE BREAKFAST RUSH. FRED'S BEHIND THE COUNTER.
MARTHA'S TAKING AN ORDER FROM DEBBIE, EARLY 20S,
ATHLETIC, LEAN.

                    DEBBIE

          Ham and cheese omelet, side of

          bacon, coffee.

                    MARTHA

          (KNOWING) Atkins diet.

                    DEBBIE

          Yes, ma'am.

                    MARTHA

          (CALLS TO FRED) Ham and cheese

          omelet, bacon.

                    FRED

          Comin' atcha.

HE CLIMBS ONTO THE DINER COUNTER.

                    (MORE)

                    FRED (CONT'D)

Yo. Yo yo. Your attention right

here, if you please. As you may

know, we're all appearing in a

half-hour multi-camera television

production.

                    MARTHA

(LOOKING PAST CAMERA) That would

explain the live audience in the

bleachers, Fred.

                    FRED

Yes it does.

THE FRONT DOOR OPENS. <u>BOB ENTERS</u>.

                    FRED (CONT'D)

What it doesn't explain is the

deplorable lack of humorous

dialogue, pratfalls and the like.

BOB SLIPS ON A BANANA PEEL AND HITS THE DECK IN A
MASTERFULLY EXECUTED BIT OF PHYSICAL COMEDY.

                    FRED (CONT'D)

I stand corrected.

                    MARTHA

So anyway --

                    FRED

So anyway, what we have here is a

little piece of situation comedy.

A simple little sample, as it

were. But lacking a certain

je ne sais quoi.

                    MARTHA

        There, you've said it. What we

        have here --

                    FRED

        Is a situation.

                    MARTHA

        Without the comedy.

CURT COMES THROUGH THE FRONT DOOR AND SLIPS ON THE BANANA
PEEL. HE TAKES OUT AN ENTIRE ROW OF TABLES ON HIS WAY
DOWN. IT'S A SIGHT TO BEHOLD.

SFX: THE O.S. AUDIENCE LAUGHS.

                    DEBBIE

        I stand corrected.

SFX: THE PHONE RINGS.

NO ONE ANSWERS IT. CURT LOOKS UP FROM WHERE HE LIES ON
THE FLOOR.

                    CURT

        Anyone gong to help me up?

                    DEBBIE

        Nope.

                    FRED

        Not a chance.

                    MARTHA

        Don't look at me. The longer

        you're on the floor, the funnier

        it gets.

SFX: THE AUDIENCE HOWLS.

CURT CLIMBS TO HIS FEET. FRED CLAPS HIS HANDS FOR
ATTENTION.

FRED

Eyes this way, people. (WAITS)

So that's about it. (TURNS TO

O.S. AUDIENCE) How'd we do?

SFX: HUGE APPLAUSE.

EVERYONE IN THE DINER STANDS, FACES THE AUDIENCE AND BOWS.

DISSOLVE TO:

APPENDIX C

Title, Cast and Sets Pages

Sample Script Pages

This is a simple title page for a spec feature script with only one writer and no source material. This is all the information that's required.

PERFECT PITCH

written by

Gretchen Pflum

12902 Hollywood Place
Burbank, CA 91505
(818) 555-9807

This is a typical title page for an episode of a television series with two writers working as a team. The title pages for both hour and half-hour series are identical.

BETTER FRED THAN DEAD

"A Simple Sample"

written by

John Gretel & Isaac Mott

JOSHUA McMANUS PRODUCTIONS
Bungalow 15
10202 W. Washington Boulevard
Culver City, CA 90232

REV. FIRST DRAFT

August 2, 2008

Rev. 07/13/08 (Blue)
Rev. 07/15/08 (Pink)
Rev. 07/16/08 (Yellow)
Rev. 07/21/08 (Green)

This is a title page for a feature film in production and includes the names of all participating writers, the draft and date, and a listing of dates and colors for all sets of revised pages included in the current draft.

12 HOURS IN BERLIN

written by

Felix Alvin Butler Jr.

revisions by

Maria Gustav
Charles Knowles-Hilldebrand
Robert Bush

current revisions by

Johan Potemkin

FINAL DRAFT

July 12, 2008
© 2008
MICHAEL GELD PRODS.
All Rights Reserved

MICHAEL GELD PRODUCTIONS
4000 Warner Boulevard
Burbank, CA 91505

NINE LIVES

"Cats Away"

CAST

KITTY

JULIO MENDEZ

HILDE SCHMIDT

FELIX SIMPSON

LIEUTENANT MARTIN

MAX

REBECCA BEAKER

GUARD #1

GUARD #2

DR. SRINIVASAN

LYLE

SAM

TODD

MRS. BRACKMAN

ROTO-ROOTER GUY

This is a cast list for an episode of a one-hour television series. The speaking characters are listed in order of appearance. It is also common to list the series regulars first, followed by the rest of the cast in order of appearance. Extras are not listed. A cast page is not numbered. Spec scripts should not include a cast page.

NINE LIVES

"Cats Away"

CAST

KITTY...................................MARSHA WILLIAMS

JULIO MENDEZ..............................ALEX GONZALEZ

HILDE SCHMIDT.........................ALISON PARMENTER

FELIX SIMPSON....................MICHAEL PAUL MILLIKAN

LIEUTENANT MARTIN.......................ANTHONY BOGNA

GUEST CAST

MAX...TIM FISH

REBECCA BEAKER............................SYLVIA SIMMS

GUARD #1................................N. KELLY LYON

GUARD #2..................................JAMES BEISE

PARKING LOT EXTRAS
POLICE HEADQUARTERS EXTRAS

A typical cast list for an episode of a half-hour television series looks like this. Character names are listed on the left and actors' names are listed on the right. The regular cast often appears in a set order, with guest cast listed in order of appearance. Extras are listed in order of appearance below the guest cast. A cast page is not numbered. Spec scripts should not include a cast page.

<u>NINE LIVES</u>

"<u>Cats Away</u>"

<u>SETS</u>

<u>INTERIORS</u>:

KENNEDY HIGH SCHOOL
   Main Office
   Science Lab
   Library
   Girls' Bathroom

NEW YORK STOCK EXCHANGE

STORM SEWERS

POLICE HEADQUARTERS
   Holding Cell
   Detectives' Bullpen

McDONALD'S RESTAURANT

STAPLES CENTER
   Escalator
   Luxury Suite
   Basketball Court
   Visitors' Locker Room

FUNERAL HOME

<u>EXTERIORS</u>:

PARK

SCHOOL PLAYGROUND

NEW YORK STOCK EXCHANGE

DUMP
   Front Gate

SOUTH L.A. STREETS

POLICE HEADQUARTERS

McDONALD'S RESTAURANT

STAPLES CENTER

CEMETERY

VENICE BEACH

This is a sets list for a one-hour television drama. Primary locations are listed in order of appearance, with secondary locations grouped beneath each primary location. A sets page is not numbered. Spec scripts should not include a sets page.

<u>NINE LIVES</u>

<u>"Cats Away"</u>

<u>SETS</u>

Teaser, Scene A   - Int. Detectives' Bullpen - Day

Act One, Scene B - Int. Kitty's Apartment - Kitchen - Night

Act One, Scene C - Int. Kitty's Apartment - Bedroom - Night

Act One, Scene D - Int. Detectives' Bullpen - Morning

Act Two, Scene E - Int. Empire State Building - Elevator -
                   Later That Day

Act Two, Scene F - Int. Detectives' Bullpen - Same Time

Act Two, Scene G - Int. Empire State Building - Lobby -
                   30 Minutes Later

Tag, Scene H   - Int. Kitty's Apartment - Night

This is an example of a sets lists for a half-hour television series. These pages, in particular, can take many forms, but virtually always each scene number or letter is listed in order along with its location, even when that means repeating locations. Sets pages are not numbered. Spec scripts should not include a sets page.

190

INDEX

ABOUT THE AUTHOR

Christopher Riley is a professional screenwriter working in Hollywood with his wife and writing partner, Kathleen Riley. Together they wrote the 1999 theatrical feature *After the Truth*, a multiple-award-winning German language courtroom thriller. The film sparked international controversy when it was released in Germany and earned its star Goetz George a best actor nomination for the prestigious European Film Award for his portrayal of Nazi doctor Josef Mengele. Since then, the husband-wife team has written scripts ranging from legal and political thrillers to action-romances for Touchstone Pictures, Paramount Pictures, Mandalay Television Pictures and Sean Connery's Fountainbridge Films.

The author worked from 1983 to 1998 in the standard-setting Warner Bros. script processing department where he learned from veteran script proofreaders and typists with decades of Hollywood experience. He rose to manage the historic studio's script operation, supplying scripts to countless projects in development and production at Warner Bros. and virtually every other studio in Hollywood. He wrote the software used by the studio to type thousands of television and feature film scripts and he served as the final arbiter of standard script format for the studio.

In addition to writing, the Rileys train aspiring screenwriters for work in Hollywood and have taught in Los Angeles, Chicago, Washington, D.C., New York and Paris. From 2005 to 2008, the author directed the acclaimed Act One Writing Program in Hollywood.

Together with their four children, the Rileys live in Los Angeles.

The author can be reached by e-mail at chrisariley@gmail.com.

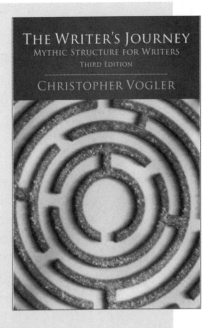

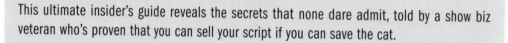

{ THE MYTH OF MWP }

In a dark time, a light bringer came along, leading the curious and the frustrated to clarity and empowerment. It took the well-guarded secrets out of the hands of the few and made them available to all. It spread a spirit of openness and creative freedom, and built a storehouse of knowledge dedicated to the betterment of the arts.

The essence of the Michael Wiese Productions (MWP) is empowering people who have the burning desire to express themselves creatively. We help them realize their dreams by putting the tools in their hands. We demystify the sometimes secretive worlds of screenwriting, directing, acting, producing, film financing, and other media crafts.

By doing so, we hope to bring forth a realization of 'conscious media' which we define as being positively charged, emphasizing hope and affirming positive values like trust, cooperation, self-empowerment, freedom, and love. Grounded in the deep roots of myth, it aims to be healing both for those who make the art and those who encounter it. It hopes to be transformative for people, opening doors to new possibilities and pulling back veils to reveal hidden worlds.

MWP has built a storehouse of knowledge unequaled in the world, for no other publisher has so many titles on the media arts. Please visit www.mwp.com where you will find many free resources and a 25% discount on our books. Sign up and become part of the wider creative community!

Onward and upward,

Michael Wiese
Publisher/Filmmaker